MONSEN AND BAER, Inc.

A Passion for Perfume Bottles

Perfume Bottle Auction XIII

May 16, 2003.

**Auctioneers: Michael DeFina
and Randall B. Monsen**

**Auction:
Hyatt Orlando Hotel
6375 West Irlo Bronson Memorial Highway
Kissimmee, Florida 34747 USA**

**Auction Preview: All lots will be available for viewing
and inspection from 10:00 AM to 5:00 PM on Friday, May 16, 2003.
Sale will begin at 5:00 PM, May 16, 2003.**

**Monsen and Baer, Inc.
Box 529
Vienna, VA 22183 USA
(703) 938-2129 Fax (703) 242-1357
email: monsenbaer@erols.com**

ISBN #1-928655-03-3

A Passion for Perfume Bottles

Table of Contents

MONSEN AND BAER PERFUME BOTTLE AUCTION THIRTEEN

Preface

To our fellow collectors in this country and abroad, greetings and good wishes! This is the thirteenth fully catalogued auction of perfume bottles produced by Monsen and Baer. This auction serves to support the International Perfume Bottle Association in that it is held during the annual IPBA Convention, and that a portion of the proceeds of the auction will be accorded to that organization. If you are a serious collector of perfume bottles, you should become a member of the IPBA, the International Perfume Bottle Association. Randall Monsen is a past president of the IPBA, and Rod Baer is currently the Publications Chair. The IPBA publishes a wonderful *Perfume Bottle Quarterly,* a Membership Directory, and organizes an outstanding annual Convention. We will happily send membership information and a sample of the *Perfume Bottle Quarterly* to all who request it.

A Passion for Perfume Bottles follows upon the success of our previous books, beginning with *The Beauty of Perfume* in 1996 and following our 2002 book, *The Joy of Collecting Perfume Bottles.* As in all our previous books, we have tried to give our readers a valuable resource for perfume bottle collecting. Over the last twelve years, Monsen and Baer publications have given collectors dozens of valuable research articles on the history of perfume companies and glass makers, in addition to photos and descriptions of thousands of perfume bottles.

A Passion for Perfume Bottles offers collectors an astonishing array of perfume bottles and atomizers by the American companies DeVilbiss, Pyramid, and Volupté, as well as an astonishing array of rarities of the commercial type, particularly in the categories of Baccarat and Lalique. The auction will finish with a tour de force of Czechoslovakian bottles.

Our overall goal in publishing books on perfume bottles is to provide the collector with a resource for collecting and research that can be used over and over again, not only on the documentation of perfume bottles and their current value, but also on their history and their makers. The hardcover book format provides a durable object for collectors to use and re-use. Our goal here goes beyond merely selling perfume bottles, though of course we wish to do that and to do it well. In a very real sense, we want to produce for collectors something that we, as collectors ourselves, would value and find useful—something we would want to own and keep on our bookshelf. Our sincere wish is that other collectors use it, learn from it, and enjoy it. What we have said in the past bears repeating here: *Knowledge–and the sharing of it–enhances the pleasure of collecting.*

We have both been collectors since early childhood—collectors of many disparate things, not just perfume bottles. A current passion for both of us is American art pottery, in particular the Roseville Pottery and other potteries of Ohio. We have spent a lot of time thinking about the art of collecting. Why do we collect? How can we have more enjoyment collecting? What advice should we give to new collectors? Collecting is an art which has as its first rule that there are no absolute rules. Each collector must decide for herself or himself what to collect and how to go about collecting it. It follows that there are as many different collections as there are collectors. Some collectors collect only commercial perfumes, some only those that are not commercial, some collect miniature perfumes, some only the larger ones. Some collect only a very specific type and others collect any-

thing they find that gives them pleasure. Nonetheless, it seems wise to us to recommend something to our fellow collectors. *First, buy books. Spend some of the collecting budget on books.* An investment in knowledge is always worthwhile, and generally the book will pay for itself in short time. Books will help one to identify objects that definitely should be acquired and others that may be passed. Books will help one avoid mistakes. But probably most important is this: knowledge increases one's pleasure, and if collecting is not about pleasure it is about nothing at all. A second piece of advice for collectors is to build quality into the collection, regardless of what type of collection it is. *Quality is more important than quantity—vastly more important.* Building quality into a collection means selecting objects of known quality and paying a fair price for them. We believe that as the twenty-first century unfolds, collectors will look back longingly and wistfully upon this sale as an opportunity to acquire incredibly desirable perfume bottles at advantageous prices. Our hope is that each collector of today will also recognize this opportunity to acquire a wonderful perfume bottle for their collection.

If you have a truly special perfume bottle that you would consider selling, then our year 2004 auction, to be held in Reston, Virginia, in May, 2004, may be the perfect venue to do so. Monsen and Baer can showcase your bottle in a book which becomes a permanent part of the literature on perfume bottles, and which can then be seen by everyone for decades to come. We also purchase bottles and sometimes entire collections directly, for those who prefer an immediate sale. For those who would like to consign bottles for the year 2004 auction, please contact us soon after this sale. Consignment details will be sent to those who request this information. The consignment deadline is December 31, 2003, but many categories fill up *long* before that date.

The collecting of perfume bottles has enriched our lives immeasurably. First, there is the excitement of discovering and purchasing each new bottle. Then there is the joy of seeing, holding, and owning these beautiful objects, a joy that never weakens or grows old. We even enjoy selling some of them, and seeing what pleasure they will give to another collector. And in addition to all this, there are many personal relationships we have developed through this wonderful hobby, and maybe that is the greatest benefit. Thus, collecting perfume bottles has given us much, and we wish in turn to strengthen and enrich this pleasureful pastime. When we began the Monsen and Baer perfume bottle auction twelve years ago, we had little idea where it would lead us, or of the vast amount of work that would eventually be required to produce a hard-cover book such as *A Passion for Perfume Bottles.* But this journey has been worthwhile, and we have grown to meet the challenges of each new year. We will continue to try to improve our publications as well as the quality of the bottles we offer for sale. We want everyone to know that we have written this book with great joy, and we sincerely hope that it will also bring enjoyment, knowledge, and a deepened appreciation of this wonderful collecting field to our fellow collectors. *To each of our readers: may your collections grow in quality, and may there be no limit to the pleasure you derive. Enjoy!*

Randy Monsen
Rod Baer

The Conditions of Sale
All lots sold in this auction are subject to the following conditions: please read carefully.

Terms of Sale. All lots will be sold, in the numerical sequence of this catalogue, to the highest bidder as determined by the auctioneer. In the case of disputed bids, the auctioneer shall have the sole discretion of determining the purchaser, and may elect to reoffer the lot for sale. We will accept cash, travelers checks, or personal checks with acceptable identification or if the buyer is known to us; we reserve the right in some cases to ship the lot to the purchaser after their check has cleared. Credit card sales are welcome.

Sales Tax. **All lots are subject to Florida state sales tax unless a valid tax exemption form has been filed with us; proof of sales tax exemption status may be required, i.e., a xerox copy of your sales tax registration form.**

Absentee Bids. A form for absentee bids is available. We will be happy to execute your bid for you as if you were present at the auction. When you do this, it does not mean that the bidding will commence with your bid, it simply means that we will not bid for you above the amount you indicate. It is advantageous to place these absentee bids as early as possible. In the case of identical bids, the bid from the floor will take precedence; for identical absentee bids, the earlier-dated bid will take precedence. Please read shipping information below. **Telephone Bids:** A very limited number of telephone lines may be available for telephone bidding. There is a $50 non-refundable fee for telephone bidding, which must be arranged two weeks prior to the auction--no exceptions.

Bidding Increments. Bidding increments are totally at the discretion of the auctioneer. However, the following increments are typically used: under $50, increments of $5; $50-$300, increments of $10; $300-$500, increments of $25; $500-$1,000, increments of $50; $1,000-$3,000, increments of $100; $3,000-$5,000, increments of $250; $5,000-$10,000, increments of $500; above $10,000, increments of $1,000.

Shipping and Handling Fees. We offer the possibility of shipping your purchases. For the United States and Canada, the flat charge for this service is **$15 per lot** for lots whose sale price is less than $1000; the charges will be higher for the lots valued over $1000 due to insurance charges. Lots which consist of large items can be shipped, with actual shipping charges to be paid by the purchaser.

Shipping purchases to Europe is also possible. **There is an initial charge of $75 for this service; additional lots will be included at the actual shipping cost, which may go above that amount if several lots are purchased.** Absentee bidders will be sent an invoice for the shipping charges and balance due; we offer the convenience of accepting payment in all major European currencies. We normally use United Parcel Service or DHL to ship to Europe, and in most cases we cannot use the Postal Service. United Parcel Service is highly reliable and extremely rapid. However, please note that the minimum charge for a small parcel sent by UPS to Europe is $75. Parcels consisting of several lots may cost twice that amount. Lots which are shipped outside the United States are subject to customs duties in the destination country, which is based upon the purchase price of the lot and we are required to state it. It is the responsibility of the purchaser to determine the amount of these duties and to pay them in full.

Price Estimates and Reserves. Some lots are offered for sale with a "reserve price." The reserve is a confidential minimum price below which the lot will not be sold. The reserve price for any lot in this sale is usually well below the low estimate and is never allowed to be higher than the estimates. The estimates are merely a range within which we believe the lot may find a buyer, but of course many lots may be sold at prices well below or well above these estimates, depending on the wishes of the bidders.

Buyer's Premium. A buyer's premium of 10% will be added to the hammer price of all lots, to be paid by the buyer as a part of the purchase price.

Condition of Lots. While we attempt to describe the condition of each lot as accurately as possible, as in all auctions, the lots here are sold "as is." We attempt to mention in the descriptions any negative aspect we think bidders need to know, for example: [label absent], [chip to stopper], etc. However, many factors relating to condition cannot be adequately described in the short captions of this catalogue, and this is especially true in the case of miniature or group lots. Very many perfume bottles have exceedingly tiny chips around the opening where the stopper enters the bottle. Sometimes these may also be found on the tongue of the stopper or on the base of the bottle. The boxes and labels of commercial bottles all show varying signs of usage and age, such as discoloration and fraying, and unless we note that the box is in pristine condition, such signs of age should be expected. All bottles, and especially commercial ones, may contain perfume residue and other internal stains. Not all stoppers fit into the bottle with perfect snugness and symmetry, especially those of Czechoslovakian manufacture. Therefore, bidders should inspect each lot they wish to bid on prior to purchase. We would also be happy to discuss the condition of any lot prior to the sale. Unless stated otherwise, the bottles are empty of perfume.

    Note on the sizes of bottles: The photographs in this catalogue depict the lots as clearly as possible. However, most photographs show the bottles *smaller* than they actually are, and some photos, especially the full page portraits, may show the bottles *larger* than they actually are. Read the lot descriptions to know the actual sizes. Measurements given in this catalogue are in inches and centimeters, rounded in most cases to the nearest quarter inch or half-centimeter.

    In cases where glass by a particular maker is described as unsigned, the catalogue can only provide a reasonable surmise, not a guarantee, as to the maker. Many of the early French glass makers produced glass of similar quality and design. In these cases, the buyer should consult the available reference works and thereafter make their own determination. The glass made by Lalique & Cie. is all grouped together; this includes bottles designed after René Lalique's death by Marc and Marie Claude Lalique. Following the convention used in Utt [1990], perfume bottles produced for sale by R. Lalique & Cie. are referred to as Maison Lalique or Cristal Lalique.

    Reference numbers are provided for Lalique, Baccarat, and in many cases for Czech glass and commercial bottles, as described in Utt [1990], Compagnie des Cristalleries de Baccarat [1986], North [1990], Forsythe I & II [1982 & 1993], Lefkowith [1994], and Leach [1997]. These reference numbers are used throughout the catalogue.

Consignments. We will be accepting consignments for our fourteenth auction, to be held May 2004, and we are particularly in search of fine perfume bottles. Our rates of consignment are very competitive with other auctions, and we can offer exposure of your bottles to a specialized buying audience. We guarantee confidentiality. We also purchase individual bottles or entire collections outright, if that avenue of sale is preferred. Contact us and we would be happy to discuss these terms with you. We are especially interested in perfume bottles of high quality, not broken or damaged pieces. Please bear in mind that consignments for the year 2004 auction must be completed by December 31, 2003 to allow sufficient time to prepare and publish the catalogue; many categories fill up well before that date.

Bibliography on the Collection of Perfume

L'Argus des Ventes aux Enchères Valentine's: Verrerie. Paris: Dorotheum Editions, 2000.

Atlas, M. and Monniot, A. *Guerlain - Les Flacons à Parfum Depuis 1828.* Toulouse, France: Editions Milan, 1997.

Atlas, M. and Monniot, A. *Un Siècle d'Echantillons Guerlain.* Toulouse, France: Editions Milan, 1995.

Ball, J. D. and Torem, D. H. *Commercial Fragrance Bottles.* Atglen, Pennsylvania: Schiffer Publishing Co., 1993.

Ball, J. D. and Torem, D. H. *Fragrance Bottle Masterpieces.* Atglen, Pennsylvania: Schiffer Publishing Co., 1996.

Barlow, Raymond E., and Kaiser, Joan E. *A Guide to Sandwich Glass: Vases, Colognes, and Stoppers.* West Chester, Pa: Schiffer Publishing, 1987.

Barille, Elisabeth. *Coty.* Paris: Editions Assouline, 1995.

Berger, C. & D. *Tous les Parfums du Monde.* Toulouse: Editions Milan, 1995.

Bonduelle, J. P. et Lancry, J. M. *Flacons à Parfums Catalogues pour les Ventes aux Enchères Publiques:* March 31, 1990; March 24, 1991; June 16, 1991; October 24, 1991; June 21, 1992; May 16, 1993; November 21, 1993; March 27, 1994; November 20, 1994; June 18, 1995; December 3, 1995; June 16, 1996; December 1, 1996; June 15, 1997; December 7, 1997; November 25, 2000; expert: J.-M. Martin-Hattemberg.

Bonhams *Scent Bottle and Lalique auction catalogues:* November 29, 1989; October 18, 1990; November 21, 1990; April 24, 1991; October 24, 1991; October 28, 1991; April 28, 1992; October 29, 1992; April 7, 1993; June 28, 1993; October 20, 1993; expert: Juliette Bogaers; September 29, 1997; experts Isobel Muston, Eric Knowles, and Emma Thommeret.

Bowman, Glinda. *Miniature Perfume Bottles.* Atglen, Pennsylvania: Schiffer, 1994.

Brine, Lynda and Whitaker, Nancy. *Scent Bottles Through the Ages: An A - Z Pictorial* Bath, UK: Brine and Whitaker, 1998.

Byrd, Joan. *DeVilbiss Perfumizers & Perfume Lights: The Harvey K. Littleton Collection.* Cullowhee, North Carolina: Western Carolina University, 1985.

Cabré, M., Sebbag, M., Vidal, V.. *Femmes de Papier - Perfumed Cards.* Toulouse: Editions Milan, 1998.

Cabré, Monique. *La Légende du Chevalier d'Orsay: Parfums de Dandy.* Toulouse: Editions Milan, 1997.

Charles-Roux, Edmonde. *Chanel and Her World.* New York: Vendome Press, 1981.

Chassaing, Rivet, Fournié. *Flacons à Parfums Catalogue pour la Vente aux Enchères Publiques.* June 27, 1994, Toulouse, France; expert: Geneviève Fontan.

Christie's South Kensington. *Lalique including the Pickard-Cambridge Collection of Lalique Scent Bottles,* May 12, 2000.

Christin, Jean. *Flacons à parfum du XXe siècle.* September 29, 1996, Hotel des Bergues, Geneva, Switzerland.

Clements, M. L. and Clements, P. R. *Avon Collectible Fashion Jewelry and Awards.* Atglen, PA: Schiffer & Co., 1998.

Cohet et Feraud *Floréal Perfume Bottle Auction Catalogue,* Toulouse, France, April 15-16, 1995; November 4, 1995; expert: Flora Entajan.

Colard, Grégoire. *[Caron] The Secret Charm of a Perfumed House.* Paris: J. C. Lattès, 1984.

Compagnie des Cristalleries de Baccarat. *Baccarat Les Flacons à Parfum/The Perfume Bottles.* Paris: Henri Addor & Associés, 1986.

Courset, J-M. *5000 Miniatures de Parfum.* Toulouse: Editions Milan, 1995.

Courset, J-M, and Dekindt, P.. *6000 Miniatures de Parfum.* Toulouse: Editions Milan, 1998.

Coutau-Bégarie, O. *Flacons à Parfums Catalogues pour les Ventes aux Enchères Publiques:* December 6, 1993; October 24, 1994; June 12, 1995; November 27, 1995; June 3, 1996; December 1, 1997; November 16, 1998; June 7, 1999; April 17, 2000; November 6, 2000; November 18, 2002; expert: Régine de Robien.

Demornex, Jacqueline. *Lancôme.* Paris: Editions du Regard, 1985.

Doyle New York. *Belle Epoque sales of February 7, 2001; June 6, 2001.* Expert: Eric Silver.

Drouot-Richelieu, Neret-Minet, Coutau-Begarie. *Flacons à Parfums Catalogues pour les Ventes aux Enchères Publiques:* June 23, 1986; April 2, 1987; Nov. 4, 1987; April 13, 1988; Nov. 7, 1988; May 20, 1989; Nov. 13, 1989; May 21, 1990; Nov. 24, 1990; April 8, 1991; May 27, 1991; Nov. 15, 1991; December 14, 1992; expert: Régine de Robien.

Drouot-Richelieu, Neret-Minet. *Flacons à Parfums Catalogue pour la Vente aux Enchères Publiques.* December 14, 1992; expert: J.-M. Martin-Hattemberg.

Drouot-Richelieu, Millon & Robert. *Flacons à Parfums: Catalogue pour la Vente aux Enchères Publiques.* December 6, 1991; expert: Régine de Robien.

Duchesne, Clarence, ed. *La Mémoire des Parfums,* Numeros 1-11. Paris, 1988-1991.

Duval, René. *Parfums de Volnay.* Catalogue of the Company, 1928.

Edwards, Michael. *Fragrances of the World 2000; Fragrances of the World 2001.* Sydney, Australia: Michael Edwards, 2000 and 2001.

Edwards, Michael. *The Fragrance Adviser 1999.* Sydney, Australia: Michael Edwards, 1999.

Edwards, Michael. *Perfume Legends: French Feminine Fragrances.* Sydney, Australia: HM Editions, 1996.

Enghien. *Flacons de Parfum.* June 22, 2002. Expert: Jean-Marie Martin-Hattemberg.

Feder, Soraya. *Divine Beauty: The Art of Collectibles.* Paris: L'Aventurine. 2001.

Fellous, Colette. *Guerlain.* Paris: Denoël, 1987.

Fleck, F. *Flacons à Parfum, Catalogue* for the Perfume Bottle Auction, March 12, 1994; expert: Anne Meter-Seguin.

Fontan, Geneviève. *Cote des Flacons de Parfum Modernes.* Toulouse: Arfon, 1999.

Fontan, Geneviève. *Cote Générale des Cartes Parfumées; Volume III.* Toulouse: Arfon, 1997, 2000.

Fontan, Geneviève. *Cote Générale des Echantillons de Parfum: Nouveautés 98; Nouveautés 99; Nouveautés 2000.* Toulouse: Arfon, 1998, 1999, 2000.

Fontan, Geneviève. *Echantillons Tubes de Parfum.* Toulouse: Arfon, 2000.

Fontan, Geneviève. *Parfums d'Extase.* Toulouse: Arfon, 1996.

Fontan, Geneviève, and Barnouin, Nathalie. *Cote Générale des Echantillons de Parfum.* Toulouse: Editions Fontan & Barnouin, 1996.

Fontan, Geneviève, and Barnouin, Nathalie. *L'Argus des Echantillons de Parfum.* Toulouse: Editions Milan, 1992.

Fontan, Geneviève, and Barnouin, Nathalie. *La Cote Internationale des Echantillons de Parfum, 1995-1996. Les Echantillons Anciens.* Toulouse: 813 Edition, 1994.

Fontan, Geneviève, and Barnouin, Nathalie. *La Cote Internationale des Echantillons de Parfums Modernes.* Toulouse: 813 Edition, 1995.

Fontan, Geneviève, and Barnouin, Nathalie. *Les Intégrales: Rochas* and *Les Intégrales: Ricci.* Toulouse: Editions Fontan & Barnouin, 1996.

Forsythe, Ruth. *Made in Czechoslovakia.* Marietta, Ohio: Richardson Printing Co., 1982; *Made in Czechoslovakia, Book 2.* Marietta Ohio: Richardson Printing Co., 1993.

Frankl, Beatrice. *Parfum-Flacons.* Augsburg: Battenberg Verlag, 1994.

Gardiner Houlgate. *Perfume Bottles, Sale 6001 [UKPBCC].* October 3, 1998. Expert: Lynda Brine.

Gerson, Roselyn. *Vintage Ladies' Compacts.* Paducah, KY: Collector Books, 1996.

Gerson, Roselyn. *Vintage and Contemporary Purse Accessories.* Paducah, KY: Collector Books, 1997.

Ghozland, F. *Perfume Fantasies.* Toulouse: Editions Milan, 1987.

Green, Annette, and Dyett, Linda. *Secrets of Aromatic Jewelry.* Paris, New York: Flammarion, 1998.

Guinn, Hugh D. *The Glass of René Lalique at Auction.* Tulsa, Oklahoma: Guindex Publications, 1992.

Hymne au Parfum: Catalogue de l'exposition, 1990-1991. Paris: Comité Français du Parfum, 1991.

Johnson, Frances. *Compacts, Powder, and Paint.* Atglen, PA: Schiffer Publishing, 1996.

Jones-North, Jacquelyne. *Czechoslovakian Perfume Bottles and Boudoir Accessories.* Marietta, Ohio: Antique Publications, 1990; revised editon, 1999.

Kaufman, William I. *Perfume.* New York: E. P. Dutton & Co., 1974.

Killian, E. H. *Perfume Bottles Remembered.* Traverse City, Michigan: E. Killian, 1989.

La Quinzaine du Parfum. Perfume Bottle Auction Catalogue for the sale of October 21, 1994; expert: Creezy Courtoy. Brussels, Belgium.

Latimer, Tirza True. *The Perfume Atomizer: An Object with Atmosphere.* West Chester, Pennsylvania: Schiffer Publishing, 1991.

Leach, Ken. *Perfume Presentation: 100 Years of Artistry.* Toronto: Kres Publishing, 1997.

Lefkowith, Christie Mayer. *The Art of Perfume.* New York: Thames and Hudson, 1994.

Lefkowith, Christie Mayer. *Masterpieces of the Perfume Industry.* New York: Editions Stylissimo, 2000.

Le Louvre des Antiquaires. *Autour du Parfum du XVIe au XIXe Siècle.* Paris: Le Louvre des Antiquaires, 1985.

Marcilhac, Félix. *R. Lalique: Catalogue Raisonné de l'Oeuvre de Verre.* Paris: Editions de l'Amateur, 1989.

Marsh, Madeleine. *Perfume Bottles: A Collector's Guide.* London: Octopus, Ltd, 1999.

Martin, Hazel. *Figural Perfume and Scent Bottles.* Lancaster, CA: Hazel Martin, 1982.

Martin-Hattemberg, Jean-Marie. *Caron.* Toulouse: Milan Editions, 2000.

Martin-Hattemberg, Jean-Marie. *Le parfum histoire et expertise, Revue Experts, #42,* March 1999.

Martin-Hattemberg, Jean-Marie. *Précieux Effluves / Scentsfully Precious.* Toulouse: Milan Editions, 1997.

Matthews, Leslie G. *The Antiques of Perfume.* London: G. Bell & Sons, 1973.

Mini Flacons. Wiesbaden, Germany: SU Verlag, 1993.

Morris, Edwin T. *Scents of Time: Perfume from Ancient Egypt to the 21st Century.* New York: Metropolitan Museum of Art, 1999.

Mouillefarine, Laurence. *Objets de la Beauté à Collectionner.* Boulogne, France: Éditions MDM, 1999.

Mueller, Laura M. *Collector's Encyclopedia of Compacts: Volumes 1 and 2.* Paducah, KY: Collector Books, 1996.

Neret-Minet. *Flacons à Parfums Catalogue pour les Ventes aux Enchères Publiques,* November 14, 1991; expert: Elisabeth Danenberg.

North, Jacquelyne. *Commercial Perfume Bottles.* West Chester, Pennsylvania: Schiffer Publishing Co, 1987.

North, Jacquelyne. *Perfume, Cologne, and Scent Bottles.* West Chester, Pennsylvania: Schiffer Publishing Co, 1986.

La Parfumerie Française et L'Art dans la Présentation. La Revue des Marques de la Parfumerie et de la Savonnerie: Paris, 1925.

Parfum, Art, et Valeur. Catalogue de Vente, November 15, 1991. Expert: Geneviève Fontan.

Paulson, Paul L. *Guide to Russian Silver Hallmarks.* Paulson: Washington DC, 1976.

Pavia, Fabienne. *The World of Perfume.* New York: Knickerbocker Press, 1995.

Perfume Bottle Quarterly, Volumes 1-15. International Perfume Bottle Association.

Phillips Auctions. *Perfume Presentations.* October 6, 1996, October 26, 1997; October 25, 1998. Geneva, Switzerland. Expert: Christie Mayer Lefkowith. *Perfume Presentations.* November 27, 1999. Zürich, Switzerland; December 10, 2000, New York. Expert: Ken Leach.

René Lalique and Cristal Lalique Perfume Bottles (The Weinstein Collection). New York: Christie's/Lalique Society of America, 1993.

René Lalique et Cie. Lalique Glass: The Complete Illustrated Catalogue for 1932. Reprinted by The Corning Museum of Glass, Corning, New York. New York: Dover Publications, 1981.

Restrepo, Federico. *Le Livre d'Heures des Flacons et des Rêves.* Toulouse: Editions Milan, 1995.

Scent Bottles Through the Centuries: the Collection of Joan Hermanowski. St. Petersburg, Florida: Museum of Fine Art, 1997.

Sloan, Jean. *Perfume and Scent Bottle Collecting.* Lombard, Illinois: Wallace-Homestead Co., 1986.

Sotheby's New York. *Important Twentieth Century Decorative Works of Art, including the Mary Lou and Glenn Utt Collection of Lalique.* New York, December 4-5, 1998.

Taylor, Pamela F. *Heavenly Scents.* Privately published, UK, 2000.

Truitt, R. and D. *Czech Glass 1918-1939. Glass Collector's Digest,* Vol. 10, #6, May 1997. pp. 39-46.

Utt, Mary Lou and Glenn. *Lalique Perfume Bottles.* New York: Crown Publishers, 1990. *Updated Addendum Listing and Photo Supplement,* 2001.

Watine-Arnault, D.. *Flacons à Parfums Christian Dior: Catalogue pour la Vente aux Enchères Publiques.* April 12, 1992; expert: Régine de Robien.

Whitmyer, M. & K. *Bedroom and Bathroom Glassware of the Depression Years.* Paducah, Kentucky: Collector Books, 1990.

Important Books Available from Monsen and Baer:

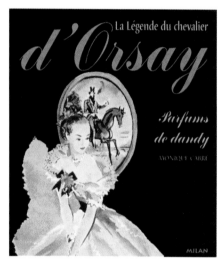

Baccarat Les Flacons à Parfum/The Perfume Bottles [Cristalleries de Baccarat] @ $85 + $9 shipping. Hardcover§

Caron [J.-M. Martin-Hattemberg] *Editons Milan* 205 pp, text in English and French. @ $69.95 + $9 shipping. Hardcover§

Guerlain: A Century of Minis: 1895-1995 [M. Atlas and A. Monniot] *Editions Milan 160 pp, text in English and French.* @ $60 + $7 shipping. Hardcover§

The Legend of the Chevalier d'Orsay: Parfums de Dandy [M. Cabré] @ $48 + $7 shipping. Text in French and in English, Hardcover§

Made in Czechoslovakia, Book 2 [R. Forsythe] @ $29.95 + $5 shipping. Softcover¶

Perfume, Cologne, and Scent Bottles [J. Jones-North] @ $69.95 + $7 shipping. Hardcover§

Perfume Legends [Michael Edwards] @ $120.00 + $8 shipping. Hardcover§

We can ship the above books to Europe, but the airmail cost is as follows: §*These books can be shipped for an additional $35 each;* ¶*These books can be shipped for an additional $18 each.*

Baccarat Les Flacons à Parfum - The Perfume Bottles
Price: $85, plus $9 shipping.

The Legend of the Chevalier d'Orsay: Parfums de Dandy, by Monique Cabré. A history of d'Orsay, beautifully illustrated, with text in English and French, Hardcover, 126 pp.
Price: $48, plus $7 shipping.

Caron by J.-M. Martin-Hattemberg. Toulouse, France: Editions Milan, 2000. Beautifully illustrated, with text in French and English, Hardcover, 205 pp.
Price: $69.95, plus $9 shipping.

Monsen and Baer publish these books on American Art Pottery:
The Collectors' Compendium of Roseville Pottery, Volumes I and II.

These books include new historical research and color photos of all the pieces in the pottery lines covered. Price guide information is included in Volume I and a separate price guide accompanies Volume II. Both books are 128 pp each, hardcover, and prices are postpaid. Volume III will be available summer 2000.

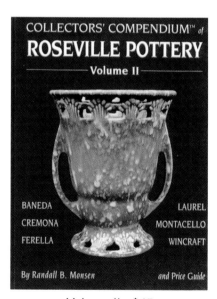

Volume I - $35

Volume II - $45

These Monsen and Baer Publications are available, all with prices realized [Shipping: $4.50 for first one, $3.00 for each additional title]:

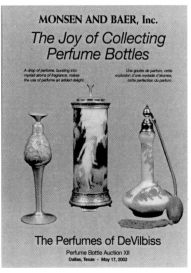

AUCTION LOTS: MINIATURES, FIRST SIZES, SOLIDS

Lot #1. Angelique *Gold Satin* clear glass bottle with white plastic top; Bourjois *Premier Muguet* clear glass bottle with flower form top; Leonard *Fashion* clear glass bottle and stopper; Revillon *Partner* clear glass bottle with white cap; Victoria's Secret *Rapture* clear glass atomizer with gold top; Paloma Picasso clear glass bottle in white holder. All six items in their original boxes. Est. $100.00-$200.00.

Lot #2. Les Meilleurs Parfums de Paris Weil *Antilope*, Worth *Je Reviens*, *Y* de Yves St. Laurent, Dana *Tabu*, Givenchy *Le De*, Balenciaga *Le Dix*, Grès *Cabochard*, Carven *Ma Griffe*, *S* de Schiaparelli, Jacques Griffe *Enthousiasme*, in their box. Est. $100.00-$150.00.

Lot #3. Bourjois *On the Wind* set: clear glass cologne bottle with orange cap, 3.7" [9.5 cm], full, orange label; miniature glass bottle and orange cap, 1.8" [4.5 cm], orange label, in a gold box with celluloid window. Est. $125.00-$200.00.

Lot #4. Unidentified maker *Key to My Heart,* clear glass bottle with key attached; DeVilbiss hexagonal bottle, label on bottom; atomizer decorated with flowers, marked *Royal Bavaria, Germany;* Cardinal *Chypre, Bouquet, Gardenia,* three bottles marked *Pat. Pending,* with labels, in their holder. Four items. Est. $75.00-$125.00.

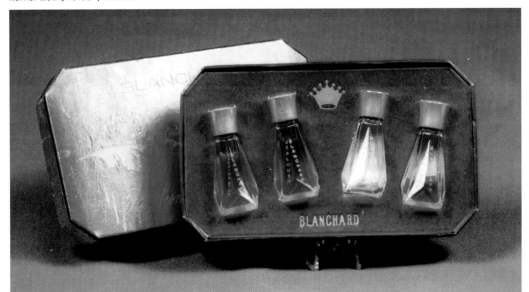

Lot #5. Blanchard *Perfume Collection* set of four clear glass bottles with gold caps: *Jealousy, Evening Star, Conflict, Intrigue,* 2" [5.1 cm], names in gold on fronts of bottles, in their red and gold box decorated with oak leaves. Est. $75.00-$125.00.

Lot #6. Ciro *Le Chevalier de la Nuit* clear glass bottle and frosted glass stopper, 2.4" [6 cm], a rare miniature replica of the standard bottle, tiny heart at center. Est. $400.00-$500.00.

Lot #7. Helena Rubenstein *Heaven Sent* miniature glass bottle and metal cap, 2.4" [6.1 cm], molded as a baby angel with wings behind, tiny label on bottom. Est. $75.00-$125.00.

Lot #8. Edhia *Tabac Doux - Cloche de la Liberté* ['Sweet Tobacco - Liberty Bell'] blue glass bottle with gold metal cap, 2" [5 cm], unopened, gold label at neck, the Liberty Bell's crack clearly drawn in gold enamel, in its box; this was probably a post World War II production intended for Americans. Est. $100.00-$150.00.

Lot #9. Lancôme *Conquete, Peut-Être, La Vallée Bleue, Bocages* clear glass bottles and frosted glass stoppers, 2.2" [5.6 cm], bottom of each bottle molded *Lancôme France,* each with its label, in their pretty box. Est. $150.00-$250.00.

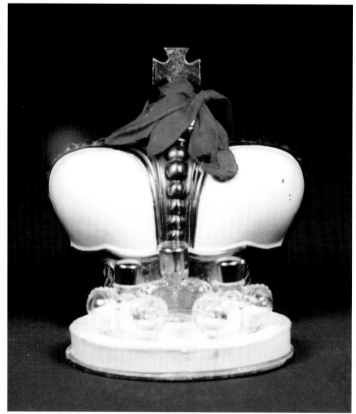

Lot #10. Matchabelli *Katherine the Great, Ave Maria, Prophesy,* clear glass bottles with brass caps, 1.3" [3.3 cm], in their white box in the shape of a crown, with red ribbon. Est. $150.00-$250.00.

Lot #11. Saville *Mischief* black glass miniature with chrome cap, 1.8" [4.6 cm], silver and black labels on front, in its pretty white plastic box lined in satin decorated with a dancing couple. Est. $200.00-$300.00.

Lot #12. Christian Dior *Poison* metal and glass bracelet, 4" diameter [10 cm], the black bracelet painted with green spots, signed *Christian Dior,* in its original box. Est. $300.00-$400.00.

Lot #13. Karoff *Barette: Chypre, Orchid, Gardenia,* three clear glass bottles with metal stoppers, made to look like bottles at a bar, Stuart label on back. Est. $100.00-$150.00.

Lot #14. Corday *Voyage à Paris* clear glass bottle and stopper, 2.3" [5.8 cm], marked *1/4 oz. size,* names in gold on front, bottom marked *Corday.* Est. $150.00-$250.00.

Lot #15. Saville *June* clear glass bottle and round black cap, 2.6" [6.6 cm], the label featuring a lady with a parasol, in its green box marked *June.* Est. $50.00-$100.00.

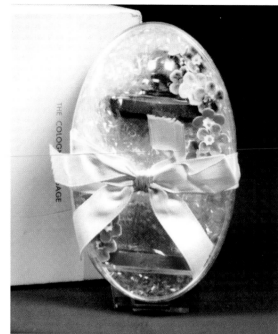

Lot #16. Caron *Les Pois de Senteur de Chez Moi,* white pouch and box; Charbert *Carnation* clear glass bottle and gold cap, in its plastic case and box; Corday *Toujours Moi* gold and clear bottle and stopper, in its box; Coty *Paris* bottle with gold cap, in gold shoe and box; Lelong *Tailspin,* in its box; Nina Ricci *L'Air du Temps,* gold vial and funnel in its box. Six items. Est. $225.00-$300.00.

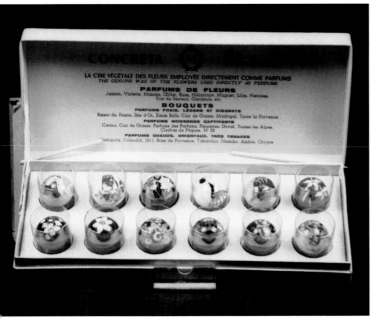

Lot #17. Molinard *Concreta* set of 12: *Ambre, Calendal, Gardenia, Habanita, Iles d'Or, Jasmin, Muguet, Narcisse, Parfum des Parfums, Pois de Senteur, Rose, Violette;* each in a clear plastic case, in their mint condition box. Est. $400.00-$600.00.

Lot #18. Fragonard *Supreme, 5, Xmas Eve,* tiny containers for solid perfume, 1.2" [3 cm], made of wood and stamped on the back *Cognac,* each with label, in their original box. Est. $100.00-$150.00.

Lot #19. Ybry *Joie de Vivre, Femme de Paris, Désir du Coeur, Palo Alto, L'Amour Toujours* set of five clear glass 'cobblestone' bottles with black caps, 2.5" [6.4 cm], labels on front and around neck, each bottle signed *Ybry* in the mold on the bottom, in their red vinyl case; Ybry bottle with frosted cap, no label, empty, *Ybry* across top of stopper. Two items. Est. $100.00-$150.00.

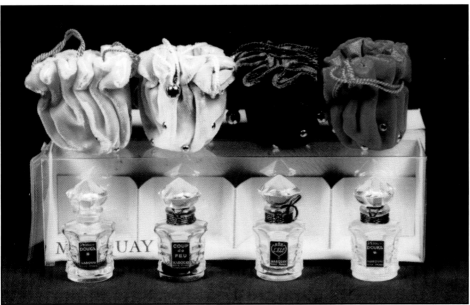

Lot #20. Marquay *Elegance de Paris: L'Elu, Prince Douka, Coup de Feu* four clear glass bottles and stoppers, each a replica miniature form, in their individual purses of red, pink, blue, and white, and in their original box. Est. $300.00-$400.00.

Lot #21. Marquay *Coup de Feu, L'Elu, Prince Douka* set of seven clear glass miniature bottles with gold caps, 1.5" [3.8 cm] each in a tiny velvet drawstring purse [black, white, violet, yellow, peach, blue, green], in their box with celluloid cover. Est. $300.00-$400.00.

Lot #22. Coty *L'Origan* perfume, eau de toilette, and *Sub-Deb* lipstick, 3.9" and 2.5" [9.9 and 6.4 cm], in a pretty presentation of two swans, bottles signed *Coty;* Corday *Toujours Moi,* 3.7" [9.4 cm]; Grès *Cabochard* clear glass bottle with frosted stopper, 2.6" [6.6 cm], in its box. Three items. Est. 100.00-$150.00.

Lot #23. Vigny *Echo Troublant* and *Heure Intime* clear glass bottles with gold stoppers, 1.8" [4.6 cm], replica miniatures, with triangular labels, in their plastic boxes marked *Vigny.* Est. $100.00-$150.00.

Lot #24. Jean Patou *Moment Supreme* clear glass bottle with gold cap, 2.4" [6.1 cm], bottle molded with cabochons, gold label on bottom and on neck, in its white box lined in blue silk. Est. $150.00-$250.00.

Lot #25. Renoir *Chi-Chi* miniature clear and frosted glass bottle with screw-on bakelite top, 2" [5.1 cm], the bottle full and sealed with a string, in its beautiful red and white box decorated with a lady in plumes. Est. $400.00-$500.00.

Lot #26. Schiaparelli *Shocking* clear glass miniature bottle with gold cap, 2.1" [5.3 cm], beautiful "S" label on front, in its pink box and gold carrier. Est. $100.00-$200.00.

Lot #27. Fabergé bath perfume *Aphrodisia* clear glass bottle and gold screw on cap, 3.4" [8.6 cm], in its hatbox like presentation with advertising pamphlet [soap lacking]. Est. $75.00-$125.00.

Lot #28. Fabergé *Tigress* clear glass bottle and stopper, 3.1" [8 cm], label around the bottle, *Fabergé* in gold letters on the stopper, in its box. Est. $100.00-$200.00.

Lot #29. Lucretia Vanderbilt *A Concentrated Extract* blue glass bottle and stopper, 2.3" [5.8 cm], front of bottle with a butterfly in silver, tiny label on bottom signed *Lucretia Vanderbilt.* Est. $400.00-$500.00.

Lot #30. Marcel Rochas *Femme* opaque white glass bottle, gold metal stopper with long dauber, 2.6" [6.6 cm], the bottle covered in black lace [small tear on one side] held in place by a gold metal spring, empty, in its black purse. Est. $300.00-$400.00.

Lot #31. Worth *Dans la Nuit* blue glass bottle and stopper of ball shape, 1.8" [4.5 cm], stopper molded with name and a crescent moon, empty. Est. $125.00-$175.00.

Lot #32. Revillon *Carnet de Bal* ['Dance Card'] clear glass bottle and stopper, 1.9" [4.8 cm], the bottle and stopper shaped as a brandy snifter inverted, empty, label on top of stopper, signed *Revillon* on bottom edge, in its green and white box; this is probably a first size. Est. $125.00-$200.00.

Lot #33. D'Orsay *Intoxication* clear glass bottle and gold metal cap resembling the pleats of a skirt, 2.2" [5.6 cm], near full, in its original box beautifully decorated with a dancing couple. Est. $125.00-$200.00.

Lot #34. Schiaparelli *Succes Fou* ['Smash Hit'], 1.6" [4 cm], the bottle of heart form emblazoned with a fig leaf, on a pin with fig leaf for wearing, in its beautiful pink and green box, with outer box. Est. $1,500.00-$2,000.00.

Lot #35. Lenthéric *Miracle* clear glass bottle and stopper with its dauber, 1.9" [4.8 cm], an indentation for the label front and back, with its box. Est. $75.00-$125.00.

Lot #36. Lancôme *Magie* clear glass bottle and brass screw-on stopper, 2.3" [5.8 cm], the square bottle with an indented patch on both sides for the label, bottom signed *Lancôme,* in its original box. Est. $75.00-$125.00.

Lot #37. Lancome *Trésor* and *Magie* clear glass bottles and stoppers, 2.9" and 2.6" [7.4 and 6.6 cm], of identical shape with flowers decorating the stoppers, some perfume, both signed *Lancôme* on the bottom. Est. $100.00-$200.00.

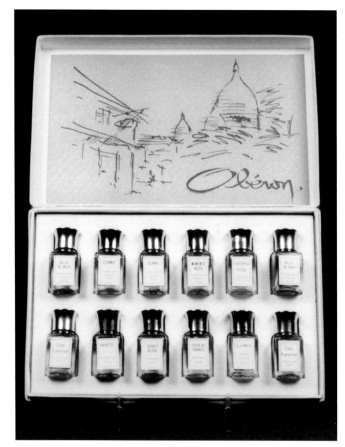

Lot #38. Fragonard *Belle de Nuit* [2], *Zizanie* [2], *Moments Volés, Gardenia Royal*, Oberon *Une Caresse* [2], Lamballe *Nanette, Source Bleue, Mercoeur Cour de France*, Carmel Myers *Gamin* set of 12 minis in identical bottles, each with gold cap and label, in their original box marked *Obéron*. Est. $100.00-$175.00.

Lot #39. Myrurgia *Joya* clear glass bottle and stopper, 1.8" [4.6 cm], the bottle of cube shape but with many facets, gold label, full, in its white and gold box lined with satin. Est. $150.00-$250.00.

Lot #40. Schiaparelli *Shocking* miniature glass bottle and metal cap, 1.9" [4.8 cm], full, tape measure label with *S* in a circle; clear glass bottle and gold cap, full, pink label, in their book-form box marked *Gift from Paris by Schiaparelli Special Edition.* Est. $200.00-$300.00.

Lot #41. United Toilet Goods Co *18th Century Old Colonial* miniature perfume bottle, 2.2" [5.6 cm], in its hurricane lamp holder with label on the shade and on the bottom. Est. $50.00-$100.00.

Lot #42. Evyan *Surprise: White Shoulders, Most Precious,* and *Great Lady,* 2.4" and 3.2" [6.1 and 8.1 cm] two rectangular bottles with gold caps, and a heart shaped bottle with gold cap, in their gold satin lined box, with outer box. Est. $100.00-$150.00.

Lot #43. Lucien Lelong *Indiscret* clear glass bottle and gold screw-on stopper, 1.9" [4.8 cm], together with a tiny promotional pamphlet and a case in which it was mailed from France. Est. $100.00-$175.00.

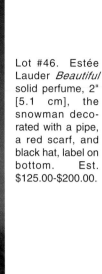

Lot #46. Estée Lauder *Beautiful* solid perfume, 2" [5.1 cm], the snowman decorated with a pipe, a red scarf, and black hat, label on bottom. Est. $125.00-$200.00.

Lot #45. Estée Lauder *pleasures* solid perfume in the shape of a champagne bottle in a bucket filled with ice, 2" [5.1 cm], the bucket engraved with the word *2000*. Est. $100.00-$175.00.

Lot #44. Colgate & Co. *Caprice* clear glass bottle and metal stopper, 3.1" [7.8 cm], label around the bottle. Est. $50.00-$100.00.

Lot #47. Estée Lauder *pleasures* solid perfume in the shape of a delicious peach, 1.7" [4.3 cm], the leaf set with a row of rhinestones, bottom with tiny label. Est. $125.00-$200.00.

Lot #48. Helena Rubenstein *Heaven Sent* solid perfume compact shaped as a shell, 1.5" [3.8 cm], unused condition, in its original box. Est. $100.00-$150.00.

Lot #49. Houbigant *Chantilly* perfume solid locket shaped as a round disk, 1.5" [3.8 cm], a variegated pattern on both sides, unused condition, in its box. Est. $100.00-$150.00.

Lot #50. Max Factor *Aquarius* gold metal perfume solid in the shape of an owl with the eyes as green stones, 1.4" [3.6 cm], empty, with loop to be worn on a gold bracelet, in its box. Est. $125.00-$200.00.

Lot #51. French perfume containers in the shape of two black men, 1.5" [3.8 cm], of Bakelite decorated with different style hats and broad smiles. Est. $150.00-$250.00.

Lot #52. Guerlain *Rachel Rosée* [*La Poudre C'est Moi*] powder box, mint condition; Chatel *Polvos de Belleza Conga* mint condition copper powder box, in its box; Lucien Lelong *Siroco,* mint condition. Three items. Est. $75.00-$150.00.

Lot #53. Sterling silver powder container, 2" [5.1 cm], black enamel and silver design; Barbara Gould powder box and rouge, signed; Bourjois powder box, signed. Est. $100.00-$175.00.

Lot. #54. Bourjois *Evening in Paris* bath dusting powder, with signed powder puff inside, never opened, the box decorated with Parisian scenes; Bourjois *Soir de Paris Ocrée* 1.2" x 2.4" [3 x 6 cm], decorated with Parisian themes, mint condition. Two items. Est. $75.00-$125.00.

Lot #55. Caron *La Nuit de Noël* black glass solid display form bottle, 7.4" [19.7 cm], of solid glass including stopper, silver and gold label. Est. $250.00-$350.00.

PERFUME LAMPS

Lot #56. Leart Art Deco perfume lamp in the shape of a woman's head, 6.5" [16.5 cm], the lips and earrings painted bright red, with original tag. Est. $100.00-$200.00.

Lot #57. Goebel perfume lamp shaped like a Chinese lantern, 7.5" [19 cm], beautifully painted in multicolors with a red and gold top, bottom signed *Goebel W. Germany*. Est. $300.00-$450.00.

Lot #58. Perfume lamp in the shape of a sitting terrier, 7.4" [18.8 cm], the dog looking downward and with a pink bow around its neck, of German manufacture. Est. $300.00-$400.00.

Lot #59. Perfume lamp in the shape of a sitting terrier, 7" [17.8 cm], newly rewired, of German manufacture. Est. $250.00-$350.00.

Lot #60. Perfume lamp in the shape of a Pierrot with violin, 7.7" [19.6 cm], the face beautifully painted in flesh tones, mold number *10021*, with original wiring. Est. $500.00-$600.00.

Lot #61. Perfume lamp molded in the shape of a polar bear standing atop the world, the globe painted in blue and brown, rewired, numbered *5265*, of German manufacture. Est. $300.00-$450.00.

Lot #62. Etling perfume lamp in the shape of a sitting Indian, 7" [17.8 cm], beautfully painted in tones of yellow and red and green, newly rewired, artist signed *Chuparus*. Est. $400.00-$600.00.

Lot #63. Very small continental brûle parfum, 5" [12.7 cm], of porcelain enameled in dark blue with Chinese vignettes, in blue and other colors. Est. $150.00-$250.00.

CROWN TOP BOTTLES

Lot #64. Perfume lamp shaped as an Oriental woman, 7.5" [19 cm], beautifully enameled in yellow, red and other colors, with a gold hat; newly rewired; of continental manufacture. Est. $300.00-$500.00.

Lot #65. Crown top perfume bottle on a powder dish, 5.8" [15 cm], the figure painted in green and red, signed with the crown over a stylized *S*. Est. $150.00-$250.00.

Lot #66. Crown top perfume bottle and stopper, 5" [12.7 cm], in the shape of a googlie-eyed cat, bottom inscribed *4739 Germany*. Est. $200.00-$300.00.

Lot #67. An adorable Schuco perfume bottle monkey, 5" tall standing [12.7 cm], the body made of mohair, in excellent condition and all original. Est. $250.00-$350.00.

Lot #68. Crown top bottle and stopper, 2.9" [7.4 cm], decorated differently on both sides with handpainted flowers, maker's mark in dark blue on bottom. Est. $100.00-$150.00.

Lot #69. Crown top perfume bottle and stopper, 3.2" [8.1 cm], shaped as a maiden holding an urn, unmarked. Est. $150.00-$250.00.

Lot #70. Porcelain bottle with metal crown stopper, 2.7" [6.9 cm], the clown holding a bouquet of flowers, beautifully molded and painted, back molded *24627*, of Bavarian manufacture. Est. $200.00-$300.00.

Lot #71. Crown top perfume bottle and stopper, 3.3" [8.4 cm], in the shape of a pierette with arms around a pole, signed *Germany 14937*. Est. $150.00-$250.00.

Lot #72. Porcelain crown top bottle and stopper, 2.9" [7.3 cm], the baby with his hands crossed behind his back, marked with the numbers *7946* and bottom marked *Germany*. Est. $200.00-$300.00.

Lot #73. German white glass perfume bottle and crown top stopper, 2.2" [5.6 cm], the goolie-eyed clown smiling, bottom marked *Germany*. Est. $125.00-$200.00.

Lot #74. Crown top bottle in the shape of a dachshund painted in reddish brown, 2.9" [7.4 cm], back signed *Germany*. Est. $100.00-$150.00.

Lot #75. Atomizer in the shape of a standing elephant, 2.4" [6.1 cm], of German manufacture. Est. $100.00-$150.00.

Lot #76. Pair of bottles: ceramic bottle and stopper, 2.6" [6.6 cm], with a butterfly and flowers; crown top bottle, 2.5" [6.4 cm], decorated with different fuschia flowers front and back. Two items. Est. $125.00-$200.00.

Lot #77. German glass bottle and metal crown top stopper, 3" [7.6 cm], the white glass decorated with swirls of gold and dark blue, unsigned. Est. $100.00-$175.00.

Lot # 79. Clear glass perfume bottle and stopper, 2.5" [6.4 cm], on a lucite stand with a white rose; lucite atomizer with a pink rose, 4" [10.2 cm]; atomizer bottle in a lucite container with an orchid, 3" [7.6 cm]. Three items. Est. $50.00-$100.00.

Lot #78. Porcelain crown top perfume bottle in the shape of a woman in a chant, 5" [12.7 cm], yellow and blue attire, with a necklace of a bull, back inscribed *24858,* of German manufacture. Est. $250.00-$350.00.

Lot #80. Victorian hand perfume bottle, 5.3" long [13.5 cm], the simple form a lady's hand with wedding ring prominently on the fourth finger, unmarked. Est. $50.00-$150.00.

Lot #81. Clear glass bottle and stopper, 6.8" [17.3 cm], of pressed glass with a starburst motif, unsigned but probably of American manufacture. Est. $100.00-$150.00.

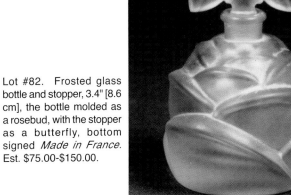

Lot #82. Frosted glass bottle and stopper, 3.4" [8.6 cm], the bottle molded as a rosebud, with the stopper as a butterfly, bottom signed *Made in France.* Est. $75.00-$150.00.

Lot #83. Roland glass scent bottle and stopper, 5.4" [13.7 cm], the outside covered with irridized gold and glass strands, the inner well in deep rose, bottom signed *Roland 8292 - 93.* Est. $100.00-$200.00.

Lot #84. Rose teinte bottle and faceted ball stopper, 6" [15.2 cm], the color gently becoming darker towards the top of the bottle, unsigned. Est. $100.00-$200.00.

Lot #85. 1930's style bottle and stopper, 6.4" [16.2 cm], of molded amber glass, stopper and bottle highlighted with golden lines, unsigned. Est. $75.00-$100.00.

Lot #86. Pressed glass perfume bottle and stopper, 3.7" [9.4 cm], the bottle molded with facets, the stopper a frosted bluebird, empty, unsigned. Est. $50.00-$100.00.

Lot #87. Pair of glass bottles and stoppers, 5.3" [13.5 cm], the bird with head down standing on a ball, unsigned but probably of American manufacture. Est. $50.00-$100.00.

Lot #88. Beautiful bottle with a very wide base 4.5" [11.4 cm], the stopper with its very long dauber shaped as a goldfish, bottom signed *36...[indistinct]...© 88.* Est. $50.00-$100.00.

Lot #89. Clear and turquoise glass bottle and stopper, 7.8" [19.8 cm], the bottle molded elaborately with scrolls and fanciwork, gold at lip, bottom signed *GH*. Est. $200.00-$300.00.

Lot #90. Glass bottle and stopper with its long dauber, 3.8" [9.6 cm], the body of the bottle decorated in pink and brown strands of glass, bottom signed indistinctly *T. Meluar.* Est. $100.00-$150.00.

Lot #91. Clear glass bottle and figural dog stopper, 4.9" [12.5 cm], the stopper a cute terrier, unmarked. Est. $100.00-$175.00.

Lot #92. Clear crystal bottle and stopper, 4.2" [10.7 cm], the round bottle inset with upward pointing leaves, bottom singed *Orrefors*. Est. $100.00-$150.00.

Lot #93. Beautiful bottle of black glass with gold inclusions, 3.5" [8.9 cm], unsigned. Est. $150.00-$200.00.

Lot #94. Cut crystal perfume bottle and stopper, 7.4" [18.8 cm], the body of the bottle cut with a cross hatching design, unsigned. Est. $100.00-$150.00.

Lot #95. Clear crystal perfume bottle and stopper, 4.7" [12 cm], both bottle and stopper designed with faceted ribs, stopper with dauber, unmarked. Est. $75.00-$125.00.

Lot #96. Turquoise blue glass perfume bottle and stopper, bottle only 6" [15.2 cm], decorated in gold with flowers and a scroll design, in an elaborated gold holder with leaves. Est. $150.00-$250.00.

Lot #97. Interesting atomizer of clear glass, 4.5" [11.4 cm], decorated with panels of leaves, unusual hallmark or maker's mark on back. Est. $200.00-$350.00.

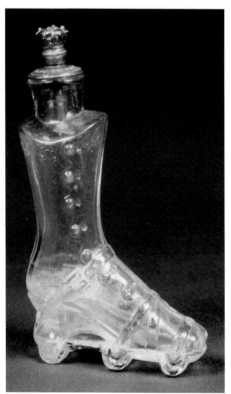

Lot #98. Solon Palmer clear glass bottle and metal crown stopper, 4.9" [12.5 cm], in the shape of a roller skating boot. Est. $100.00-$200.00.

Lot #99. Swarovski brilliant crystal bottle and stopper, 2.8" [7.1 cm], faceted with triangles and with a brilliant turquoise neck, signed with the Swarovski swan. Est. $100.00-$150.00.

Lot #100. Clear glass bottle and stopper, 5.3" [13.5 cm], the stopper molded as a bird, unsigned. Est. $25.00-$50.00.

Lot #101. Victorian era glass bottle with blue serpent and stopper, 6.9" [17.5 cm], the serpent decorated with gold dots and complete to its tail, country of origin unidentified. Est. $300.00-$450.00.

Lot #102. Lundberg Studios clear glass perfume bottle and stopper with long dauber, 6" [15 cm], the thick glass internally decorated with daffodils, side signed *Steven Lundberg Lundberg Studios 1991 - 030124.* Est. $200.00-$300.00.

Lot #103. Clear glass powder jar and cover, 5.4" [13.7 cm], the top molded with a Scottish terrier, unsigned. Est. $75.00-$125.00.

Lot #104. Lundberg Studios perfume bottle and stopper with long dauber, 7.3" [18.5 cm], blossoms in white against dark blue, bottom signed *Lundberg Studios 1990, 03/208,* side signed *Daniel Salazar* and *Steven Lundberg.* Est. $300.00-$400.00.

Lot #105. Silver overlay bottle and stopper, 5.6" [14.2 cm], a design of overlapping church windows, unsigned. Est. $200.00-$300.00.

Lot #106. Pair of clear glass bottles and stoppers, 2.7" [6.9 cm], the top of the bottles and the stoppers decorated with gold leaves and berries. Est. $100.00-$200.00.

Lot #107. Pretty little bottle of bell form, 4.4" [11.2 cm], decorated with hand-painted flowers in white and red, unsigned. Est. $75.00-$125.00.

Lot #108. Interesting bottle of pyramidal form, 5.5" [14 cm], the bottle decorated with an overlay of red crystal in geometric Art Deco fashion, conforming stopper, bottom marked *Made in France for Saks Fifth Avenue*. Est. $300.00-$400.00.

Lot #109. Moser amber glass bottle and stopper, 3.7" [9.4 cm], of rectangular shape with an indented design, bottom signed *Moser Karlsbad*. Est. $350.00-$450.00.

Lot #110. Silver overlay perfume bottle and stopper, 5.1" [13 cm], with beautiful overlay encasing the entire bottle, tongue of stopper with small bruise, unengraved condition. Est. $300.00-$450.00.

Lot #111. Clear glass bottle and stopper with silver deposit, 4.2" [10.7 cm], both bottle and stopper covered nicely with a design of leaves and flowers, unsigned. Est. $150.00-$200.00.

Lot #112. Clear glass perfume bottle and stopper, 4.9" [12.4 cm], with its glass dauber, an elaborate frieze of metal flowers extending around the bottle, unsigned. Est. $100.00-$175.00.

Lot #113. Beautiful Bohemian crystal bottle and stopper, 4.9" [12.5 cm], basically four sided with many decorative forms, unsigned. Est. $200.00-$350.00.

Lot #114. Clear glass scent bottle mounted with chains as a brooch, 1.6" [4 cm] height of bottle alone, the front covered in metal filigree and decorated with a blue stone, stopper with glass dauber and also with a blue stone. Est. $100.00-$150.00.

Lot #115. Violet cut to clear bottle and stopper with silver overcap, 3.3" [8.4 cm], cut in beautiful fashion. Est. $400.00-$600.00.

Lot #116. Vigny *Le Golliwogg* rare black perfume pin, 1" [2.5 cm], shaped as a golliwogg's head. Beautiful condition and *very rare*. Est. $200.00-$300.00.

Lot #117. Beautiful quality clear glass bottle, 4.9" [12.5 cm], decorated with geometric motifs in black and frosted glass, silver collar with British hallmarks, unsigned. Est. $200.00-$350.00.

Lot #118. Beautiful bottle commemorating an unknown fair or exposition, each side a reverse painted panel showing different views of the exposition, on a chain. This is an exquisite bottle. Est. $450.00-$550.00.

Lot #119. Deep green glass bottle with metal atomizer attachment mounted on a functioning music box, 8.4" [21.4 cm], the perfume well internally enameled in black, the exterior with an Art Deco design in gold enamel, new ball and tassel, unsigned. Est. $500.00-$600.00.

Lot #120. Translucent turquoise glass bottle and metal atomizer, 6.7" [17 cm], the exterior wheel-cut with a flower and leaf design enameled in gold, new ball and cord, unsigned. Est. $200.00-$300.00.

Lot #121. Light amber glass bottle with metal atomizer attachment, 6.3" [16 cm], the perfume well internally enameled in black, decorated with gold, new atomizer ball, unsigned. Est. $150.00-$250.00.

Lot #122. Beautiful blue cut back to clear atomizer bottle, probably French, 7" [17.8 cm], the body formed of eight rows of cut ovals, bulb lacking, unsigned. Est. $200.00-$300.00.

Lot #123. Beautiful blue cut back to clear atomizer, 5.6" [14.2 cm], beautifully cut with a pinwheel design, atomizer bulb lacking, unsigned. Est. $100.00-$200.00.

Lot# 124. Atomizer of greenish color glass, 5.7" [14.5 cm], decorated with three different panels of nudes dancing, with original atomizer ball, unsigned. Est. $150.00-$250.00.

Lot #125. Italian green and white glass atomizer, 3.5" [8.9 cm], the green and white stripes coming down the bottle, unsigned. Est. $100.00-$175.00.

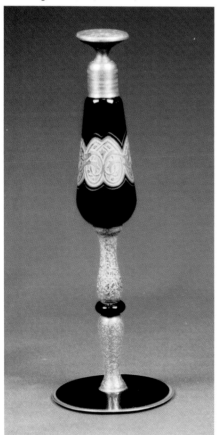

Lot #126. Statuesque black glass bottle with metal neck and glass dropper, 9" [22.8 cm], etched with an Arabesque design and enameled in gold, unsigned, dropper top impressed with flowers. Est. $600.00-$800.00.

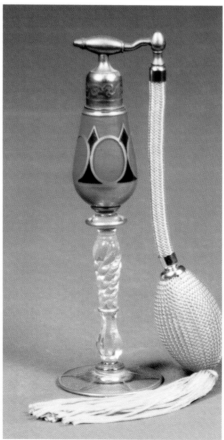

Lot #127. Volupté clear glass bottle and metal atomizer, 7" [17.8 cm], pedestal base with a twisted stem, internally enameled in mauve, the exterior in black and gold enamel, with label marked *24 kt gold plated* and signed *Volupté* in gold. Est. $400.00-$500.00.

Lot #128. Colorful atomizer of multicolored glass, round shape, 5.5" [14 cm], metal signed *Marcel Franck, Made in France, Brevete SGDG*. Est. $100.00-$150.00.

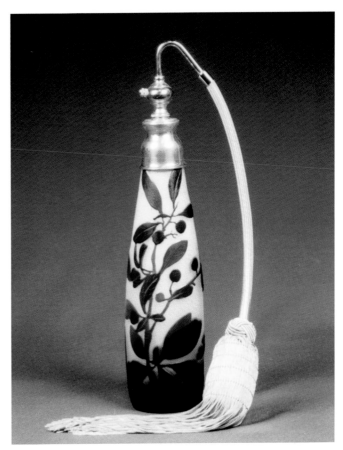

Lot #129. Beautiful atomizer with a painted scene of birds flying against a reddish sky, top marked *Marfranc, Patented France,* new bulb. Est. $1,000.00-$1,250.00.

Lot #130. Gallé dark reddish over light green glass atomizer, 9.7" [24.6 cm], with a design of leaves and berries, new atomizer attachment, signed *Gallé* on the side. Est. $1,500.00-$2,000.00.

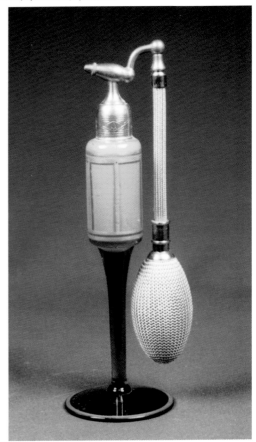

Lot #131. DeVilbiss glass bottle with metal atomizer, 7.5" [19 cm], the perfume well in orange, the exterior in gold with an abstract design, new ball and tassel, bottom signed *DeVilbiss* in black enamel. DeV #K-20 [1927]. Est. $300.00-$400.00.

Lot #132. DeVilbiss glass bottle with metal atomizer, 7.2" [18.2 cm], the ovoid bottle enameled in blue with a stenciled design of flowers in black, original atomizer ball and cord [hardened], signed *DeVilbiss* in enamel. DeV #D-51 [1928]. Est. $200.00-$300.00.

Lot #133. Light amber glass bottle with metal atomizer attachment, 7.5" [19 cm], the columnar perfume well enameled internally in deep opaque yellow, new cord and atomizer ball, unsigned. Est. $200.00-$300.00.

Lot #134. DeVilbiss dresser ensemble consisting of tray, 2 covered boxes, and an oval pin dish, the bottom of the tray painted gold, small pin dish signed *DeVilbiss*. Est. $300.00-$450.00.

Lot #135. DeVilbiss glass powder jar and cover, 4.5" [11.4 cm], decorated in orange and gold with a gold and black money plant design on the top, unsigned. Est. $300.00-$400.00.

Lot #136. DeVilbiss glass powder jar and cover, 4.7" [11.9 cm], the inside enameled in a coral pink, the cover stenciled with an abstract design in black enamel, unsigned, DeV #VS-303 [1928]. Est. $100.00-$175.00.

Lot #137. DeVilbiss Lenox porcelain penguin with atomizer made for DeVilbiss, 4.4" [11.2 cm], the black felt cape conceals the atomizer bulb and the sprayer is the penguin's nose, bottom signed *DeVilbiss* in green enamel and *Lenox USA.* Est. $300.00-$450.00.

Lot #138. DeVilbiss pair of glass bottles, one with atomizer, one with dropper, tallest 7" [17.8 cm], enameled in light blue, original ball with crocheted cover, bottom of both signed *DeVilbiss* in gold enamel and one with black *DeVilbiss* label. Est. $450.00-$650.00.

Lot #139. DeVilbiss elegant pair of black glass bottles with silver metal mounts, tallest 6.5" [16.5 cm], one with atomizer attachment, one with glass dauber, new atomizer ball, unsigned. DeV #E/DE-21 [1926]. Two items. Est. $400.00-$600.00.

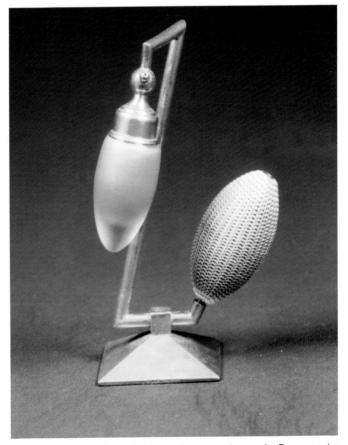

Lot #140. DeVilbiss frosted glass bottle mounted on an Art Deco angular frame with new atomizer bulb at one end, the bottle enameled internally in green, total height 6" [15.2 cm], unsigned. DeV #513 Debutante Series [1928]. Est. $500.00-$600.00.

Lot #141. DeVilbiss mauve powder box and dresser tray: rectangular glass tray, 7" x 10.3" [17.7 x 26 cm], enameled pink on the bottom and carved with leaves, the top enameled in gold with a flower design, unsigned; elegant powder jar of conforming design, 5.6" [14.2 cm], bottom signed with *DeVilbiss* paper label. Two items (one below). Est. $250.00-$350.00.

[Lot 141]

Lot #142. Green glass dropper bottle, 2.5" [6.4 cm], plain squat form, bottom signed *DeVilbiss*. Est. $75.00-$150.00.

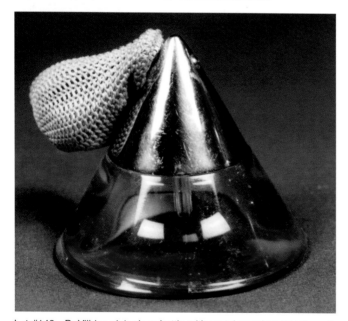

Lot #143. DeVilbiss pink glass bottle with metal atomizer attachment, 2.5" [6.4 cm], designed as a cone, original [hardened] ball, bottom signed *DeVilbiss* with a paper label also marked *Patent Pending*. DeV #S100-118 [1934]. Est. $150.00-$250.00.

Lot #144. DeVilbiss diminutive clear glass bottle with chrome metal atomizer attachment, 2.2" [5.6 cm], of square shape, in its original black leather case stamped *DeVilbiss* in silver. DeV #S650-8 [1936]. Est. $250.00-$350.00.

Lot #145. DeVilbiss set of three deep pink-enameled items: oval glass tray, 10.8" [27.4 cm], covered powder jar [small chip or burst bubble], 4.2" [10.7 cm] diameter; atomizer bottle, 6.5" [16.5 cm]; all three items trimmed with black enamel, bottle signed *DeVilbiss* in gold and impressed *DeVilbiss* on metal neck. Three items. Est. $350.00-$450.00.

Lot #146. DeVilbiss chrome metal atomizer, 5.4" [13.7 cm], molded with a band of stylized flowers at the top, some losses to chrome around base, bottom with a *DeVilbiss* paper label marked *Patent 2162756 2189229.* Est. $200.00-$300.00.

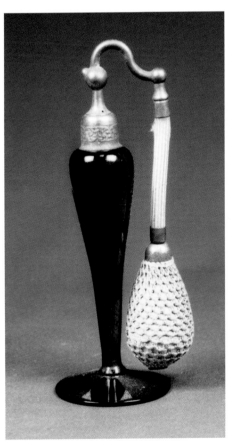

Lot #147. DeVilbiss black glass bottle with metal atomizer attachment, 6.7" [17 cm], the black glass embedded with gold inclusions, original ball with crocheted cover, bottom signed *DeVilbiss* in gold. DeV #G-21 [1927]. Est. $250.00-$350.00.

Lot #148. DeVilbiss frosted glass atomizer bottle with gold metal overcap, 5.2" [13.2 cm], the cylindrical bottle molded with forget-me-nots, the overcap with its original tassel, bottom signed *DeVilbiss* in acid and with silver label. DeV #S750-21 [1936]. Est. $250.00-$350.00.

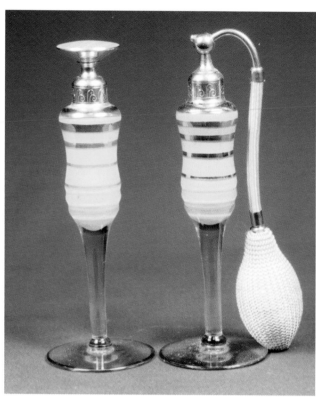

Lot #149. DeVilbiss amber glass ginger jar with atomizer, 6.3" [16 cm], with a pine needle design in gold, signed *DeVilbiss* in acid. DeV #S800-6 [1937]. Est. $500.00-$650.00.

Lot #150. DeVilbiss yellow glass bottle and metal atomizer, 6.7" [17 cm], an elongated egg shape, original ball [hardened], signed *DeVilbiss* in gold enamel. Est. $175.00-$250.00.

Lot #151. DeVilbiss pair of glass bottles, one with metal atomizer attachment, one with dropper, tallest 6.5" [16.5 cm], the perfume wells internally enameled in yellow, the exteriors decorated with bands of gold enamel, unsigned. DeV #BDB-78 [1926]. Est. $400.00-$500.00.

Lot #152. DeVilbiss atomizer bottle, 7" [17.8 cm], internally enameled in orange, fancifully decorated on the outside with black leaves and gold, apparently unsigned. Est. $400.00-$600.00.

Lot #153. DeVilbiss perfume lamp of blue glass, 5.2" [13.2 cm], black bands at bottom of globe, unsigned. Est. $250.00-$350.00.

Lot #154. DeVilbiss cranberry swirled glass bottle and stopper with long dauber, 6.3" [16 cm], stopper in gold, red, and yellow, bottom signed *DeVilbiss* in gold enamel. Est. $300.00-$400.00.

Lot #155. Art glass tray in superb condition, fanciful flowers painted and enameled in green, black, orange and gilded, 7" x 10.25" [17.8 x 26 cm], bottom signed *DeVilbiss*. Est. $300.00-$500.00.

ot #156. DeVilbiss glass perfume bottle with metal atomizer, 7.5" [19 cm], internally enameled in green, the exterior etched and enameled in gold and black with a star design on the pedestal and an unusual petal design on the well, new ball, bottom signed *DeVilbiss* in gray enamel. DeV #K-18 [1926]. Est. $350.00-450.00.

Lot #157. DeVilbiss clear glass bottle with metal atomizer top, 8.2" [20.8 cm], the bottle decorated with triangular windows surrounded by gold etching, the pedestal bearing a flower design, new atomizer ball, metal signed *DeVilbiss*. Est. $350.00-$450.00.

Lot #158. DeVilbiss light green glass perfume bottle, 6.6" [16.8 cm], internally decorated in green and enameled on the outside with gold bands [some wear to one band], in its original green box decorated with black and silver Art Deco motifs. DeV #B-76 [1930]. Est. $250.00-$350.00.

43

Lot #159. DeVilbiss perfume atomizer and powder jar, 7" [17.8 cm] and jar 4.5" diameter [11.4 cm], enameled black internally, gold decor on outside, original atomizer ball, in its original box signed *DeVilbiss*. Est. $200.00-$300.00.

Lot #160. DeVilbiss opaque aqua glass bottle with metal atomizer attachment, 6" [6.1 cm], new ball and tassel, metal neck impressed *DeVilbiss*. DeV #F-11 [1924]. Est. $200.00-$300.00.

Lot #161. Gold Aurene atomizer bottle of short form, 6.2" [15.8 cm], beautiful goldish blue color, original atomizer ball, unsigned. Est. $500.00-$600.00.

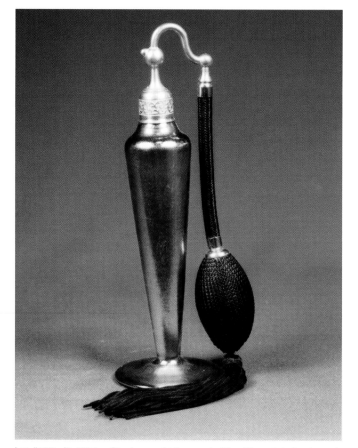

Lot #162. DeVilbiss glass bottle with a metal atomizer attachment, 7.8" [19.8 cm], the perfume well internally enameled in black, the exterior decorated in acid-etched gold and with orange enamel, new ball and tassel, bottom signed [faintly] *DeVilbiss* in enamel. DeV #L-26 [1927]. Est. $450.00-$600.00.

Lot #163. DeVilbiss Steuben gold Aurene bottle with metal atomizer attachment, 7.5" [19.1 cm], of trumpet form on a pedestal base, new ball and tassel, unsigned. Est. $600.00-$800.00.

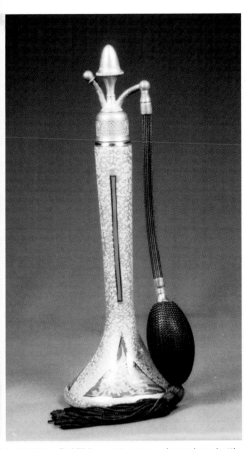

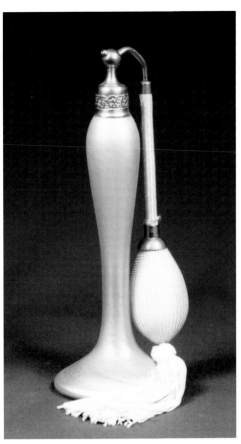

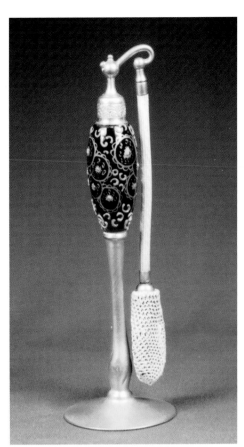

Lot #164. DeVilbiss statuesque clear glass bottle and gold metal atomizer with gold acorn finial, 9.8" [24.9 cm], decorated with gold, wheel-cut with a design of birds and flowers, new ball, unsigned. Est. $700.00-$800.00.

Lot #165. DeVilbiss yellow gold irridescent satin glass bottle with metal atomizer attachment, 7.5" [19 cm], new ball and tassel, unsigned, glass by the Quezal company. DeV #K-14 [1927]. Est. $700.00-$900.00.

Lot #166. DeVilbiss extremely tall glass atomizer bottle, 9.5" [24.1 cm], in coral and gold with an abstract design, very minor wear to gold, original atomizer ball, signed *DeVilbiss* in gold enamel. Est. $1,000.00-$1,250.00.

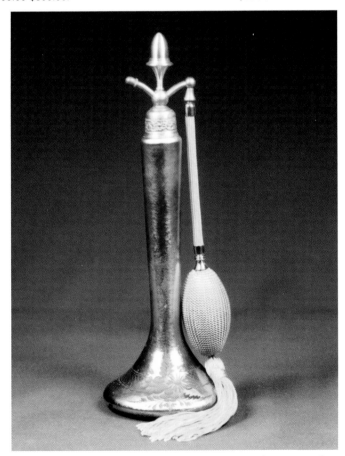

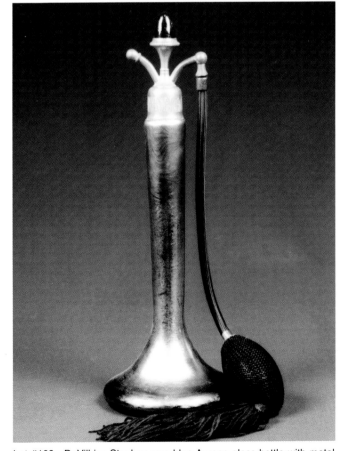

Lot #167. DeVilbiss statuesque gold, rose and blue Aurene atomizer bottle with gold acorn finial, 9.5" [24 cm], brilliant color to the glass, tiny nick to the glass, new ball and tassel, bottom signed *DeVilbiss*. Est. $800.00-$1,000.00.

Lot #168. DeVilbiss Steuben rare blue Aurene glass bottle with metal atomizer attachment and acorn finial, 9.5" [24 cm], the glass of irridescent turquoise throughout, new atomizer ball and tassel, bottom unsigned. Est. $800.00-$1,000.00.

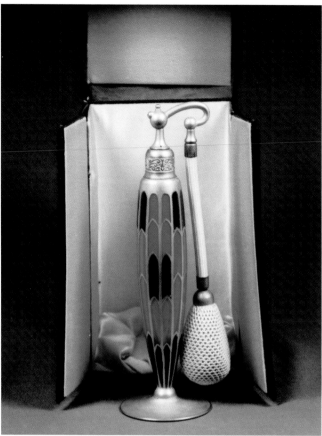

Lot #169. Lovely quality DeVilbiss perfume atomizer, 7.2" [18.3 cm], internally enameled in bright orange, the exterior enameled with abstract design in gold and black, in its very rare box lined with light orange satin with *DeVilbiss* label. Est. $800.00-$1,200.00.

Lot #170. DeVilbiss pair of cranberry glass bottles, one with metal atomizer attachment, one with glass dropper, tallest 7.5" [19.1 cm], with a scroll design on the middle and base in gold, original ball, bottom of both signed *DeVilbiss* in gold. A stunningly beautiful pair of bottles. DeV #LDB-25 [1927]. Est. $800.00-$1,200.00.

Lot #171. DeVilbiss Imperial glass atomizer, all original, in light blue and yellow, 6.8" [17.3 cm], the body set with violet jewels, bottom signed *DeVilbiss*. Est. $3,750.00-$4,250.00.

Lot #172. DeVilbiss Imperial series green glass atomizer, 7" [17.8 cm], the glass shading from light to dark and entirely encased in a gold metal frame, new atomizer ball and tassel, bottom signed *DeVilbiss* in black enamel. Est. $3,750.00-$4250.00.

Lot #173. Beautiful cameo glass bottle with silver stopper, 6.2" [15.8 cm], the outer layer of violet glass outlines lilies against a color of irridescent amber, new stopper, unmarked. Est. $800.00-$1,000.00.

Lot #174. L. T. Piver *Pompeia Concentré* clear crystal perfume bottle shaped as a cigarette lighter, 2.5" [6.4 cm], inner stopper with its dauber, names in gold, bottom signed *Baccarat*. Est. $300.00-$450.00.

Lot #175. Marcel Franck atomizer, 5.4" [13.7 cm], enameled with a flower basket design front and back, bulb lacking, bottom signed *MF Baccarat*. Est. $200.00-$300.00.

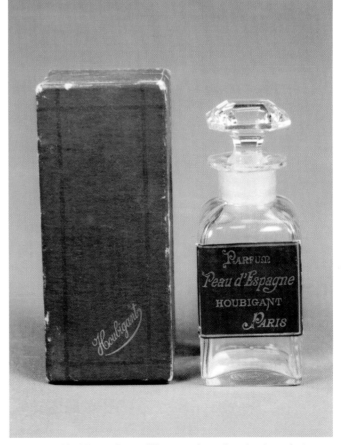

Lot #176. Lubin *L'Ocean Bleu* clear crystal bottle and stopper, 6.1" [15.5 cm], two dolphins with a hole at center, empty, signed *Baccarat;* designed for the Paris 1925 Exposition des Arts Decoratifs. Est. $700.00-$900.00.

Lot #177. Houbigant *Peau d'Espagne* clear glass bottle and stopper, 4.1" [10.4 cm], of decanter shape, beautiful gold and dark red label, in its matching box; bottom signed *Baccarat*. Est. $350.00-$450.00.

Lot #178. Molyneux *Charm* clear crystal bottle and stopper, 5.9" [15 cm], of simple and elegant apothecary shape with a disc stopper, label on front, signed *Baccarat*. Bacc. #524 [1940]. Est. $200.00-$300.00.

Lot #179. Christian Dior *Miss Dior* clear crystal bottle and stopper of amphora shape, 7" [17.8 cm], empty, bottom signed *Baccarat* in emblem. Bacc. #814 [1949]. Est. $500.00-$600.00.

Lot #180. D'Orsay *Le Chevalier* clear crystal bottle and stopper, 4.1" [10.5 cm], empty, with an especially beautiful gold label; bottom signed *Baccarat*. Bacc. #10 [1912]. Est. $300.00-$400.00.

Lot #181. Dealer's sign of triangular shape, 3.2" x 1.5" [8.1 x 3.8 cm], Baccarat emblem on bottom. Est. $125.00-$175.00.

Lot #183. Corday *Orchidée Bleue* very large size bottle and stopper, 3.5" [8.9 cm], both bottle and stopper molded with a flowerform motif, label lacking around shoulder of the bottle, empty, signed *Baccarat* in emblem. Bacc #591 [1925]. The Baccarat edition of this bottle is rarely seen. Est. $300.00-$400.00.

Lot #182. Guerlain *Coque d'Or* ['Bow of Gold'] blue glass bottle and stopper, 3.1" tall [7.9 cm], in the form of a bowtie, covered in gold enamel, names in black enamel on either side, empty, signed *Baccarat* with the emblem on bottom. Bacc. #770 [1937]. Est. $650.00-$800.00.

Lot #184. Sumptuous bottle by Georges Chevalier for Baccarat, 5.7" [14.4 cm], the heavy bottle enameled in gold and decorated with blue and red flowers and black leaves, unsigned, by Baccarat. This was made for the Baccarat exhibit at the 1925 World's Fair in Paris. Est. $2,000.00-$3,000.00.

Lot #185. L. T. Piver *Astris* clear crystal bottle and stopper, 4.7" [12 cm], of decanter shape, the entire bottle encased in a metal frame bearing the label on front, empty, glass spritzer attachment, bottom signed *Baccarat*, in its very rare velvet-lined wood case. Bacc. #398 [1919]. Est. $2,000.00-$2,500.00.

Lot #186. Houbigant *Le Parfum Idéal* clear crystal bottle and stopper, 4.2" [10.7 cm], Art Nouveau gold label on front depicting a lady smelling a blossom, some perfume, signed *Baccarat* with paper label, in its colorful fabric box. Bacc. #10 [1907-1923]. Est. $250.00-$350.00.

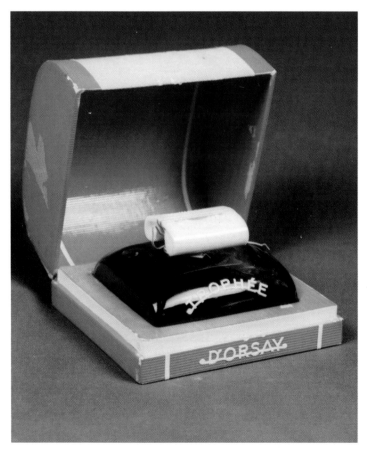

Lot #187. D'Orsay *Trophée* clear crystal bottle and white crystal stopper, 2.7" [6.9 cm], of inkwell shape with a stopper bearing the D'Orsay coat of arms, full and sealed, label on front, bottom signed *Baccarat* in emblem, in its yellow and white box. Bacc. #757 [1935]. Est. $600.00-$750.00.

Lot #188. Elizabeth Arden *It's You* clear and frosted crystal bottle and stopper, 6.2" [15.7 cm], a hand holding a vase, blue enameled rose stopper, empty, signed *Baccarat*. Bacc #781 [1939]. Est. $1,250.00-$1,750.00.

Lot #189. Mury *Patricia* superb crystal bottle and stopper, 3.9" [9.9 cm], full and sealed, enameled entirely in gold and hand-painted with a poppy in pink, in its beautiful box, gently faded; beneath the gold on the bottom the Baccarat insignia can be seen. Bacc. #618 [1926]. Est. $15,000.00-$20,000.00.

Lot #190. Bruyere *En Attendant* ['While Waiting'] clear crystal bottle and stopper, 4.1" [10.4 cm], an octagonally shaped bottle, with its label, signed *Baccarat* on the bottom. Est. $200.00-$300.00.

Lot #191. Ybry *Mon Ame* ['My Soul'] violet crystal over white atomizer, 3.2" [8.1 cm], perfectly rectangular, signed in acid on bottom *Ybry Paris Made in France.* Est. $350.00-$500.00.

Lot #192. Ciro *Danger* unusual clear crystal bottle, inner stopper, and black crystal overcap, 3.2" [8.1 cm], some perfume, bottom signed *Baccarat* in emblem. Bacc. #777 [1938]. Est. $250.00-$350.00.

Lot #193. Houbigant *Un Peu d'Ambre* clear crystal bottle and stopper, 4.2" [10.7 cm], an overall architectural shape, empty, label on front, unsigned. Bacc. #415 [1919]. Est. $300.00-$400.00.

Lot #194. Christian Dior *Diorissimo* clear crystal bottle of urn form and stopper with bronze doré flowers, 8.7" [22 cm], names faintly in gold, bottom signed *Baccarat.*. Bacc. #819 [1955]. Est. $2,000.00-$2,500.00.

Lot #195. Neiman Marcus Co. unidentified fragrance clear glass bottle and frosted stopper, 4.1" [10.4 cm], with an Art Deco label and gold stopper, signed *Baccarat.* Bacc. #596 [1926]. Est. $400.00-$500.00.

Lot #196. Lubin *Magda* clear crystal bottle and frosted glass stopper, 5.2" [13.2 cm], the stopper a maiden with gilded flowers, full and sealed, label in gold, signed *Lubin Paris.* Est. $4,000.00-$6,000.00.

Lot #197. Jean Desprez *Etourdissant* ['Stunning'] clear crystal bottle and stopper, 3.7" [9.5 cm], with perfume and sealed, *Baccarat* emblem + label on base. Bacc. #111 [1911]. Est. $200.00-$300.00.

Lot #198. Rimmel *Vocalise* clear crystal bottle, inner stopper, and overcap, 3.9" [9.9 cm], the bottle of octagonal column form, some perfume, names in gold enamel in inset letters, in its silk lined red box, signed *Baccarat* on base. Bacc. #522 [1923]. Est. $750.00-$1,000.00.

Lot #199. Marcel Guerlain *Kadour* clear crystal bottle and stopper, 4.5" [11.4 cm], the stopper of umbrella shape, empty, gold and black label on front, bottom signed *Crystal Nancy* in circle emblem, in its box covered in paper simulating burl oak; circa 1920's. Est. $600.00-$750.00.

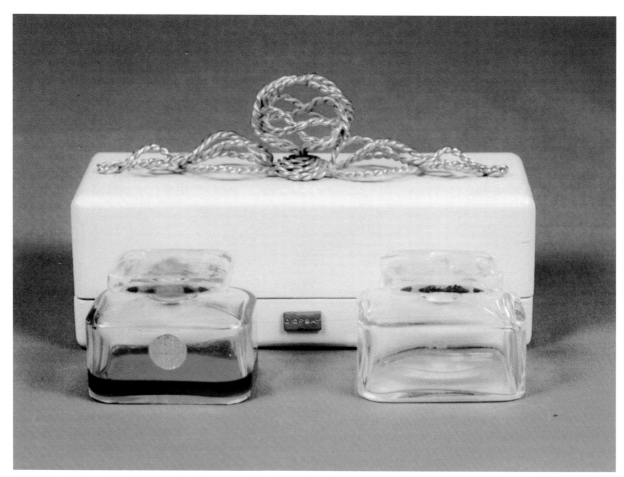

Lot #200. D'Orsay *Duo Mystère* pair of clear crystal bottles and stoppers, 1.7" [4.3 cm], of short rectangular form with stoppers of conforming shape, the portrait of the Count d'Orsay in 19th century attire molded into the stopper, empty, unsigned, in their unusual wood box with D'Orsay metal tag and elaborate wire decoration. Bacc. #793 [1944]. Est. $500.00-$600.00.

Lot #201. Jean Patou *Joy* clear crystal bottle and stopper, 2.7" [6.8 cm], the bottle enameled gold at top and at bottom, signed *Jean Patou* and *Baccarat* on the bottom, in its original box and outer box. Est. $750.00-$900.00.

Lot #202. Molyneux *Rue Royale* clear crystal bottle and stopper, 4.3" [10.9 cm], label on front, bottom signed *Baccarat*, in its beautiful box with scenes of Paris in the 1930's. Bacc. #524 [1940]. Est. $300.00-$400.00.

Lot #203. Jean Patou *Amour Amour* clear crystal bottle and stopper, 3.5" [8.9 cm], empty, gold and blue labels, bottom signed *Jean Patou* in acid, in its cream and gold box. Bacc. #531 [1924]. Est. $700.00-$850.00.

Lot #204. Verlayne *Attente* ['The Wait'] clear crystal bottle and stopper, 2.6" [6.6 cm], empty, label on front, in its original white and gold box, bottom signed *Baccarat* in emblem. Bacc. #801 [1945]. The name may refer to World War II, then in its final stage. Est. $250.00-$350.00.

Lot #205. Ciro *Surrender* clear glass bottles and stoppers, 4" and 4.7" [10.2 and 12 cm], designed to resemble a faceted gemstone, labels on the shoulders of the bottle, empty, bottom signed *Baccarat* in emblem. Two items. Est. $400.00-$500.00.

Lot #206. Godet fragrance unidentified but possibly *Nuit d'Amour* ['Night of Love'] clear crystal bottle and frosted glass stopper, 6" [15.2 cm], the base shaped as the maidens skirt, the stopper as the woman's upper body, the maiden enraptured with the smell of roses, bottom signed *Baccarat*, label on front. Est. $17,500.00-$22,500.00.

Lot #207. American Druggists Syndicate *Jockey Club* clear glass bottle and heart-shaped stopper, 4.6" [11.6 cm], of hexagonal form, full and sealed, pretty label, in its oval box lined in red silk. Est. $200.00-$300.00.

Lot #208. Bourjois *Kobako* frosted glass bottle and stopper, 2.6" [6.6 cm], molded as an oriental snuff bottle, empty, metallic label, signed *Bourjois*, in its red and black inro box with chrysanthemums. Est. $450.00-$600.00.

Lot #209. Rigaud *Mary Garden* clear glass bottle and stopper, 4.5" [11.4 cm], sealed with some perfume, labels on bottom and front, in its red silk box with tiny pamphlet inside. Est. $400.00-$500.00.

Lot #210. Michelle Rohmer *Paradis* clear glass bottle and black glass stopper, 3.4" [8.6 cm], full and sealed, in its red box lined in red satin. Est. $100.00-$175.00.

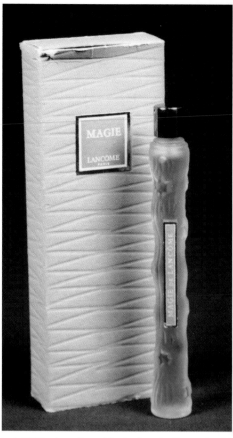

Lot #211. Avon *Vintage Year Sweet Honesty* Cologne, 5.7" [14.5 cm], a green glass bottle shaped as a bottle of champagne, full and sealed, 1979. Est. $40.00-$80.00.

Lot #212. Richard Hudnut *Three Flowers* frosted and clear glass bottle and stopper, 6.6" [16.7 cm], empty, gold metallic label showing the rose, the violet and the lily. Est. $100.00-$150.00.

Lot #213. Lancôme *Magie* glass bottle and gold cap, 5.0" [12.7 cm], an abstract design of stars on the bottle and frosted, with label, full, in its beautiful gray box. Est. $200.00-$300.00.

Lot #214. Ralph Lauren *Safari* clear glass bottle and inner glass stopper and silver cap, 4" [10.2 cm], full and sealed, initials in center of bottle, label on bottom, in its original box. Est. $150.00-$250.00.

Lot #215. Cher *Uninhibited* smokey glass perfume bottle and frosted and clear stopper, 5.2" [13.2 cm], a fantasy bottle, full and sealed, with silver chains around the neck, in its original box. Est. $100.00-$175.00.

Lot #216. Robert Piguet *Brigand* clear glass bottle and stopper, 2.6" [6.6 cm], square with a column stopper, label says this is identical to *Bandit* in Europe, in its original box. Est. $75.00-$125.00.

Lot #217. Raquel *Orange Blossom* fragrance crackle glass bottle and black glass stopper, 6" [15.2 cm], gold label on the front top of the bottle, empty. Est. $100.00-$150.00.

Lot #218. Christian Dior *Miss Dior* clear glass bottle and stopper, 3.6" [9.1 cm], of amphora shape, near full and sealed with white bow, in its white satin-lined box. Est. $125.00-$200.00.

Lot #219. Jonteel unidentified perfume frosted glass bottle and stopper, 3.7" [9.4 cm], the bottle molded with a bird and the name on front, full and sealed, in its box signed *Jonteel*. Est. $150.00-$250.00.

Lot #220. Marie Earle *Ballerina* clear glass bottle and stopper, 3.2" [8.1 cm], enameled in gold, name on top, empty, signed *Marie Earle*, in its beautiful box with gold tassel, and outer box. Est. $300.00-$400.00.

Lot #221. Unidentified maker *Encharma* oval glass bottle and partially frosted stopper, 3.6" [8.9 cm], gold label at the center of the bottle. Est. $100.00-$150.00.

Lot #222. Unidentified commerical bottle, inner stopper, and overcap, 2.8" [7.1 cm], lovely quality but unmarked. Est. $75.00-$125.00.

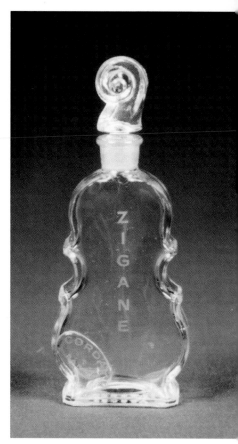

Lot #223. Corday *Ziganie* clear glass bottle and stopper in the shape of a violin, 4.4" [11.2 cm] names in gold enamel on front, bottom signed *Corday.* Est. $150.00-$225.00.

Lot #224. Jivago *Mother's Golden Love* clear glass bottle and stopper, 2.6" [6.6 cm], a square bottle with a molded heart, label on bottom. Est. $150.00-$200.00.

Lot #225. Wolf Frères *My French Cousin* clear glass bottle and stopper, 3.5" [8.9 cm], label on front, gold mark on top of stopper, empty. Est. $50.00-$100.00.

Lot #226. Degas *Danseuse Etoile* ['Star Dancer' clear glass bottle and stopper, 4.1" [10.4 cm], both bottle and stopper molded with a feather motif, bottom signed *Degas France.* Est. $75.00-$125.00.

Lot #227. Langlois *Duska* red glass bottle and black glass stopper, the large size, 4.4" [11.2 cm], designed with an architectural skyscraper motif, empty, impressed *France* on bottom. Est. $300.00-$400.00.

Lot #228. Schiaparelli *Shocking* clear glass bottle and stopper, 3.7" [9.5 cm], stopper of cube form, with its bright red label, half full, in its pink box. Est. $100.00-$175.00.

Lot #229. Lionceau perfume unidentified red glass bottle and stopper, 2.5" [6.4 cm], the oval bottle molded front and back with leaves, label lacking, bottom signed *Lionceau.* Est. $300.00-$400.00.

Lot #230. Suzy *Ecarlate de Suzy,* 4.5" [11.4 cm], in the shape of a woman's head with a hat with flower and red ribbon, names in decal, bottom with gold label. Est. $400.00-$500.00.

Lot #231. Caron lot of 4: *French Cancan* clear glass bottle with plastic cap, 3" [7.6 cm]; *Les Pois de Senteur de Chez Moi* clear glass bottle and stopper, 4.5" [11.4 cm], in its box; *Le Tabac Blond,* 3.3" [8.4 cm], label partially lacking, in its tasseled box; *N'aimez Que Moi,* clear glass bottle and stopper, 3.2" [8.1 cm], in its box. Four items. Est. $300.00-$400.00.

Lot #232. Molyneux *Le Parfum Connu,* small size bottle of rectangular form, 2.4" [6.1 cm]; this bottle was named *The Known Perfume* after the company was sued by Chanel—it had previously been called *Le Numéro Cinq, The Number Five.* Est. $50.00-$100.00.

Lot #233. Langlois *Shari* clear glass bottle and frosted glass stopper, 3.4" [8.6 cm], the bottle of octagonal form, the stopper beautifully molded with flowers, with its label, empty, in its silk box decorated with an oriental tree and birds. Est. $200.00-$300.00.

Lot #234. Unidentified maker *Royal Paris* clear glass bottle and stopper, 3" [7.6 cm], in a faceted bottle marked *Czechoslovakia* on the bottom, in its original box. Est. $125.00-$175.00.

Lot #235. Lancôme *Magie* clear crystal bottle, inner stopper, and overcap, molded in the shape of a gently twisted column, 4.6" [11.7 cm], with its gold label on top, in its sumptuous box of pink silk interior, ivory exterior with painted starburst and sequins. Est. $500.00-$650.00.

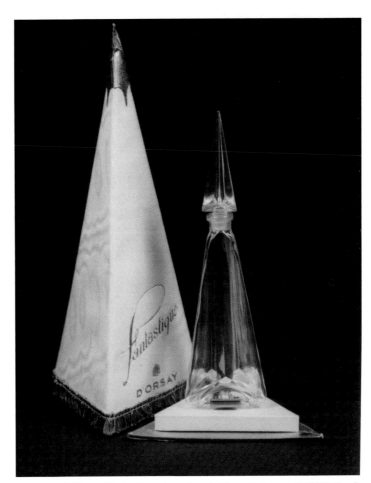

Lot #236. D'Orsay *Fantastique* clear glass bottle and stopper, 5.4" [13.7 cm], the bottle of elongated pyramid form with a sharply pointed stopper, empty, gold label, in its box , bottom signed *D'Orsay* in acid; circa 1952. Est. $400.00-$500.00.

Lot #237. Matchabelli *Royal Gardenia* frosted glass bottle and stopper, 3.8" [9.6 cm], a very large size molded in the shape of a crown, label on bottom, empty. Est. $150.00-$250.00.

Lot #238. Caron *Voeu de Noel* ['Christmas Wish'] opalescent white glass bottle and stopper, 3.6" [9.1 cm], empty, the front molded with a pair of open flowers, the stopper as a small bar, name in gold enamel on front, stopper signed *Caron* in gold. Est. $600.00-$750.00.

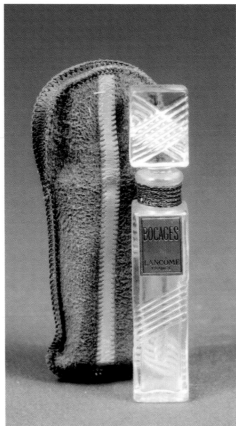

Lot #239. Colgate *Lilac* clear and frosted glass bottle and green glass stopper, 3.7" [9.5 cm], all sides of the bottle decorated with leaves and partially frosted, names at the top right corner, empty, signed *Made in France.* Est. $100.00-$150.00.

Lot #240. Lancôme *Bocages* ['Groves of Wood'] rectangular glass bottle and stopper, 3.5" [8.9 cm], the bottle and stopper molded with a band of lines, gold label, empty, bottom signed *Lancôme,* in its green case. Est. $100.00-$200.00.

Lot #241. Miss Jackson's *No. 8* black glass bottle and stopper, 3.4" [5.9 cm], of rectangular form, stopper and a design of flowers enameled gold, names in gold on bottom. Not seen in the printed literature. Est. $200.00-$300.00.

Lot #242. Lancôme *Magie* clear glass bottle and gold cap, 3.5" [8.9 cm], a teardrop with names on the cap, in its red and gray box. Est. $150.00-$250.00.

Lot #243. Jeanne Lanvin *Arpège,* rather large size black bottle with ribbed stopper, 3.7" [9.4 cm]; Lanvin logo on the front and label on the bottom. Est. $100.00-$200.00.

Lot #244. Neiman Marcus *NM* clear glass bottle and stopper, 1.7" [4.3 cm], of square form, label on top of stopper and on bottle, in its original box. Est. $100.00-$175.00.

Lot #245. DuBarry *Seven Winds* clear glass bottle and frosted glass stopper, 2.6" [6.6 cm], empty, names in gold enamel on the stopper and front of the bottle, in an unusual peach and cream box. Est. $150.00-$250.00.

Lot #246. Renoir *ChiChi* clear and frosted glass bottle and bakelite cap, 3.8" [9.7 cm], the bottle shaped as a heart resting on its side, the cap designed as the end of an arrow, unopened with its red label around neck, in its box bottom. Est. $250.00-$350.00.

Lot #247. Ciro *Doux Jasmin* octagonal bottle with a ball stopper, 3" [7.6 cm], label at center, in its brown box. Est. $75.00-$125.00.

Lot #248. Unidentified perfumer *C'est Le Moment*['The Moment is Here'] clear glass bottle and ball stopper, 4.5" [11.4 cm], the bottle designed as a square pillar, name in white enamel on front, with perfume, ruffle around neck, in its red flocked box. Est. $150.00-$250.00.

Lot #249. Berins *Number One* clear glass bottle and stopper, 2.7" [6.9 cm], the stopper as a crown, full and sealed, back signed *Ch de Berins* in gold, in its suede box with a miniature scarf. Est. $200.00-$300.00.

Lot #250. Vigny *Fleur Celeste* ['Heavenly Flower'] clear glass bottle with glass stopper and brass overcap, 2.3" [5.8 cm], label at center, empty, in its black case. This is a rare fragrance. Est. $400.00-$500.00.

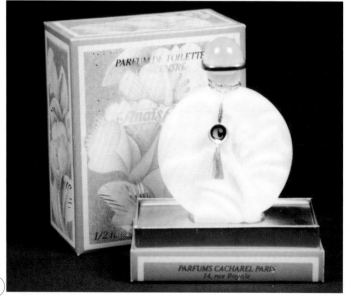

Lot #252. Caron *Nuit de Noël* ['Christmas Night'] beautful black glass bottle and stopper, 4.3" [10.9 cm], button stopper, gold label, in its early box of gold and shagreen, unsigned. Est. $200.00-$300.00.

Lot #253. D'Orsay *Mystere* clear glass bottle and stopper, 3.5" [8.9 cm], gold label at center, full of perfume, in its original box. Est. $100.00-$200.00.

Lot #251. Parfums Cacharel *Anaïs Anaïs* white glass bottle and stopper with a pink stone, 2.8" [7.1 cm], the stopper a molded flower, in its box decorated with flowers. Est. $50.00-$75.00.

Lot #254. Houbigant *Présence* clear glass bottle and stopper, 3.5" [8.9 cm], an interesting design in which the sides of the bottle curve, sealed but near empty, name in gold enamel on front, signed *Houbigant* in the mold on bottom, in its box decorated with cut ribbon, with outer box. Est. $175.00-$275.00.

Lot #255. Fath *Fath's Love* clear glass bottle and stopper, 4" [10.2 cm], empty, gold label on front, in its green flocked box. Est. $150.00-$250.00.

Lot #258. Richard Hudnut *Le Debut Noir* exceedingly tiny black glass perfume bottle and stopper, 1.3" [3.3 cm], labels on front and bottom. Est. $250.00-$350.00.

Lot #256. Dralle *Tula* clear glass bottle and frosted glass stopper, 1.7" [4.3 cm], sealed and half full, in its box marked *Made in Germany.* Est. $50.00-$100.00.

Lot #257. Vivienne *Narcisse* clear glass perfume bottles and frosted glass stoppers, 3.7" and 3.4" [9.4 and 8.6 cm], painted in green, white and violet with an design of flowers, empty, in their black box. Est. $200.00-$300.00.

Lot #259. Lancôme *Magie* clear glass bottle and frosted and clear stopper, 3.5" [8.9 cm], full and sealed, label on front, bottom signed *Lancôme France*. Est. $75.00-$150.00.

Lot #260. Lucien Lelong *Sirôcco* clear glass bottle and stopper, 3.4" [8.6 cm], molded as interlocking swirls of glass, some perfume and sealed, label near base, in its cream-colored box. Est. $125.00-$175.00.

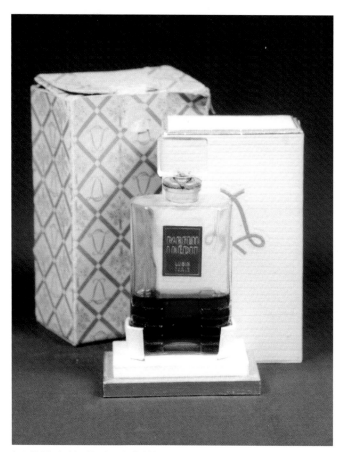

Lot #261. Lubin *Parfum Inédit* ['Unpublished Perfume'] clear glass bottle and stopper, 3.5" [8.9 cm], of rectangular form with molded geometric motifs, gold label in its white and gold box and outer box. Est. $125.00-$200.00.

Lot #262. Moiret *Le Prestige* black glass bottle and stopper, 4.2" [10.7 cm], with a fishscale motif, empty, silver label on front [some letters faint] bottom signed *France*, in its velvet-lined box marked *Moiret New York*. Circa 1940's. Est. $200.00-$300.00.

Lot #263. Caron *French Cancan* clear glass bottle and white cap, 3" [7.6 cm], the bottle molded with rings and with a skirt like ruffle around the cap, names on cap, empty, in its drop-front box lined in white and decorated with Cancan dancers. Est. $150.00-$250.00.

Lot #264. Condal *Fantasia* rare light blue glass bottle and black cap, 2.9" [7.4 cm], the bottle molded with an abstract Art Deco design and enameled in gold and blue, empty, label on bottom, in its box signed *Parfums Condal Paris.* Est. $350.00-$450.00.

Lot #265. Paquin *En Musique: Ever After, 9 x 9, Habit Rouge* three clear glass bottles with gold faceted tops, each 2.5" [6.3 cm], in their blue music box, still functioning after all these years. Est. $200.00-$300.00.

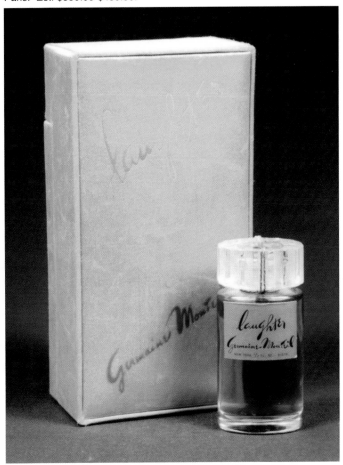

Lot #266. Germaine Monteil *Laughter* clear glass bottle with clear and frosted stopper, 2.8" [7.1 cm], the bottle of oval form, the stopper with scalloped edges, full and sealed, gold label on front, in its yellow satin box. Est. $175.00-$250.00.

Lot #267. Helena Rubenstein *Gala Performance* clear glass bottle and stopper, 5.8" [14.7 cm], molded in the shape of a woman dancing with hands aloft, the neck of the bottle formed as the woman's waist and bodice, empty. Est. $450.00-$550.00.

Lot #268. Ciro *Le Chevalier de la Nuit* huge frosted glass bottle, 7.4" [18.8 cm], in the stylized shape of a knight, black patina, unsigned. Est. $300.00-$400.00.

Lot #269. Maggie Rouff *Euphorie* clear glass bottle with frosted glass stopper, 5.6" [14.2 cm], the bottle of flat oval form, bottom signed *Rouff Paris Cannes France*. Est. $125.00-$200.00.

Lot #270. Elizabeth Arden *On Dit* ['So They Say'] frosted glass bottle and inner stopper with overcap, 4.3" [10.9 cm], molded with a design of two women whispering to each other, empty. Est. $500.00-$650.00.

Lot #271. Lucien Lelong *Jabot* frosted glass bottle and stopper with overcap, 2.7" [6.9 cm], the entire bottle in the shape of an elaborate bow of frosted and clear glass, inner stopper with long dauber, decal label on front and on bottom, empty. Est. $300.00-$400.00.

Lot #272. Woodworth *Garden Fragrance* frosted glass bottle and stopper, 5.3" [13.5 cm], the stopper molded with a large butterfly, empty, label on front. Est. $100.00-$200.00.

Lot #273. Unidentified maker, unidentified perfume frosted glass duck, 4.3" [10.9 cm], the bird is realistically molded, empty. Est. $200.00-$300.00.

Lot #274. Schiaparelli *Zut* ['Damn!!'] glass bottle and stopper in the shape of a woman's torso from the waist downward, 4.9" [12.4 cm], detail enameled in gold, gold stopper with *Zut* in green, minute fleck to stopper, bottom signed *Schiaparelli Paris*. Est. $300.00-$400.00.

Lot #275. Chanel *No 5* clear glass bottle and stopper, an older version, 2.3" [5.8 cm], in its box marked *Size 8; No. 5,* size 5N, also and older model, 3.5" [8.9 cm]; *No. 5, Cuir de Russie, Bois des Iles, No. 22,* each in an identical bottle, 2.2" [5.6 cm], in their box. Est. $75.00-$125.00.

Lot #276. Lenthéric *Three Silent Messengers - A Bientôt, Tweed, Confetti* three clear glass bottle with gold caps, 3.7" [9.4 cm], bottom of each bottle signed *Lenthéric,* in their round box. Est. $75.00-$100.00.

Lot #277. Gourielli *Five O'Clock* clear glass bottle with inner stopper and brass overcap molded as a cocktail shaker, 3.5" [9 cm], full and sealed, in its box. Circa 1947; Gourielli was the husband of Helena Rubenstein. Est. $200.00-$300.00.

Lot #278. Marcel Guerlian *Chypre* clear glass bottle and black glass stopper, 2.6" [6.6 cm], gold label on front, in its black box. Est. $100.00-$200.00.

Lot #279. Lenthéric *Miracle* clear and frosted glass bottle and stopper, 2.3" [5.8 cm], an Art Deco design with a symmetrical swirl motif, empty, labels front and back, in its stage-like box presentation. Est. $150.00-$250.00.

Lot #280. Guerlain *L'Heure Bleue* clear and frosted glass bottle and stopper, 6.5" [16.5 cm], labels on front and bottom, Mexican tax stamps on the reverse. Est. $100.00-$175.00.

Lot #281. Unidentified perfumer and fragrance frosted glass bottle and stopper, 3" [7.6 cm], shaped as a sitting cat, empty, black stain and nice detail to face, with a red ribbon around neck. Est. $300.00-$500.00.

Lot #282. Unknown maker *Rue Royale* glass bottle and stopper, 4" [10.2 cm], molded with a frosted band of leaves, bottom acid signed *Made in France*. Est. $100.00-$200.00.

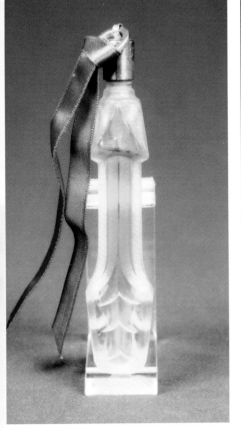

Lot #283. Lancome *Fleches* ['Arrows'] interesting frosted and clear glass arrow with metal cap, 5" [12.7 cm], name on the brass cap, full of perfume. Est. $100.00-$150.00.

Lot #284. Lilly Daché *Drifting* clear glass bottle and stopper, 5" [12.7 cm], faceted stopper, labels at neck and around the base of the bottle, on its box bottom. Est. $125.00-$200.00.

Lot #285. Karoff *PAR-fumes* set of three clear glass bottles with metal caps, each 5.9" [15 cm], molded as golf clubs, all in their red plaid golf-caddy bag with a gold foil label attached to the cords. Est. $250.00-$350.00.

Lot #286. Guerlain *Parure* clear glass bottle and smokey glass stopper, 5.7" [14.5 cm], full and sealed, name around stopper, bottom stamped *Guerlain 1974*, in its original turquoise box. Est. $150.00-$225.00.

Lot #287. Weil *Antilope* clear glass bottle and stopper, 3.9" [9.9 cm], full and sealed, label on front, *"W"* inscribed on stopper, in its box. Est. $150.00-$200.00.

Lot #288. Weil *Cassandra* clear glass bottle and stopper, 3" [7.6 cm], designed in the shape of a classical Ionic column, full and sealed, gold label on front, in its brown and cream box with Greek key motif. Cassandra was the famous clairvoyant of classical mythology. Est. $400.00-$500.00.

Lot #289. Myurgia *Maderas de Oriente* ['Oriental Wood'] clear glass bottle and stopper, 4.3" [10.9 cm], of cylinder shape, colorful label, empty, in its wooden box marked with the names burned into the wood and decorated with a green and blue wool braid. Est. $125.00-$175.00.

Lot #290. Marshall Field & Co. *Turquoise* clear glass bottle, inner stopper and overcap, 3" [7.6 cm], parts of the bottle molded in brilliant blue, bottom acid signed with names. Est. $300.00-$400.00.

Lot #291. Bourjois *Evening in Paris* blue glass bottle and frosted glass stopper, 2.7" [6.8 cm], silver label on front, in its blue star-form box. Est. $150.00-$250.00.

Lot #292. Rimmel [Paris] *Parfum Art Moderne* rectangular bottle in light green glass with a semi-circular black floral stopper, 3.4" [8.6 cm], label in front, in its original box. Est. $600.00-$750.00.

Lot #293. Mury *Le Narcisse Bleu* clear glass perfume bottle and stopper, 2.2" [5.6 cm], the front and top of the bottle molded with flowers and patinated blue, label on front, half full and sealed, in its original box. Est. $600.00-$750.00.

Lot #294. Jacques Fath *Iris Gris* ['Gray Iris'], clear glass bottle and stopper, 5" [12.7 cm], of pleated shape with a round pedestal base and pointed stopper, with perfume and sealed, gold label on front, bottom signed *Jacques Fath* in the mold, in its gray flocked box signed in gold *Jacques Fath*. Circa 1952. Est. $200.00-$275.00.

Lot #295. Jacques Heim *J'Aime* ['I Love'] clear glass bottle and stopper, 4.5" [11.4 cm], both bottle and stopper molded with ribs, empty, white label on front, bottom signed *Jacques Heim* in the mold, in its box decorated with foxes. Est. $200.00-$300.00.

Lot # 296. Caron *Royal Bain de Champagne* clear glass bottle and white screw on cap, 5" [12.7 cm], full and sealed, having the appearance, with its labels, of a champagne bottle, in its original box. Est. $200.00-$300.00.

Lot #297. Lancôme *Cuir* ['Leather'] clear glass bottle and stopper, 3.6" [9.1 cm], the stopper etched with flowers on both sides, empty, in its box decorated with orchids and arrows. Est. $100.00-$150.00.

Lot #298. Smarza *Konsuello* clear glass bottle and stopper designed with triangular facets, 6" [15.2 cm], an elegant tall shape, empty, in its antique gold box; the back of the box is labeled *Riga* [Latvia], when it was still part of the former USSR. Est. $150.00-$250.00.

Lot #299. Coty *Muse* clear glass bottle and inner stopper with frosted glass overcap, 4.1" [10.4 cm], empty, gold label on front, bottle signed *Coty,* in its satin lined box with gold florentine exterior. Est. $250.00-$350.00.

Lot #300. Whitmore *Un Pois de Senteur* ['A Sweet Pea'] black glass bottle and stopper, 3.7" [9.4 cm], the bottle decorated with purple bands, gold stopper, label and box marked *Whitmore Omaha Paris*. Est. $300.00-$400.00.

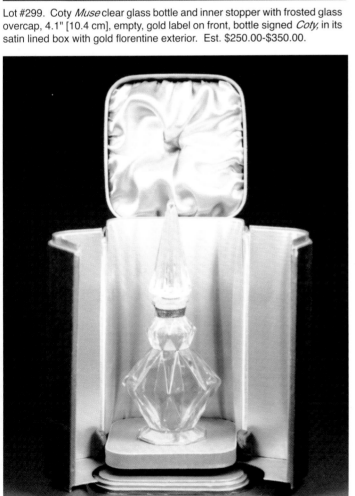

Lot #301. Jacques Fath *Fath de Fath* beautiful faceted crystal bottle and stopper, 6.5" [16.5 cm], full and sealed, the bottle cut in an eight pointed star motif, in its original box. Est. $700.00-$850.00.

Lot. #302. Seely *Lily of the Valley* beautiful hand enameled bottle with a rose in green, red, and gold, 5.2" [13.2 cm], label around neck, in its beautiful box decorated with pink flowers. Est. $350.00-$450.00.

Lot #303. Schiaparelli *Shocking Eau de Cologne* clear glass bottle with pink plastic stopper, 5.2" [13.2 cm], full, pink and white *S* label on front; *Shocking* perfume metal-clad purse bottle, 2.7" [6.9 cm], in their pink and blue box marked *Gift from Paris.* Est. $150.00-$250.00.

Lot #304. D'Orsay *Intoxication* clear glass bottle and stopper of a pleated, star-like shape 5" [12.7 cm], gold label hangs from a white cord at neck, empty, in its original pink and black box decorated with hearts, bottom signed *D'Orsay* in a circle. Est. $300.00-$400.00.

Lot #305. Jean Dessès *Kalispera* [Greek: 'Good Evening'] clear glass bottle and stopper, 4.5" [11.4 cm], the bottle designed with concave ribs, name in enamel on the top of the stopper, empty, in its elegant box of cream and red, bottom signed *JD* in the mold. Est. $350.00-$450.00.

Lot #306. Francois Gérard *Nuit de Gala* ['Gala Night'] clear glass bottle and gold cap, 2.5" [6.4 cm], gold label on top, in its elegant evening purse and red flocked box. Est. $200.00-$300.00.

Lot #307. Coty *Asuma* frosted glass bottle and stopper, 2.7" [6.9 cm], of ball shape molded with flowers, stopper molded with tiny leaves, empty, bottom signed *Coty France* in the mold, in its gold and Chinese red box decorated with oriental motifs. Est. $600.00-$750.00.

Lot #308. Corday *Kai Sang* black glass bottle and stopper, 2.9" [7.4 cm], the shape resembling an Oriental inkwell, empty, gold enamel decor of leaves, stopper enameled in Chinese red, white and gold with abstract symbols, label on shoulder. Est. $1,000.00-$1,200.00.

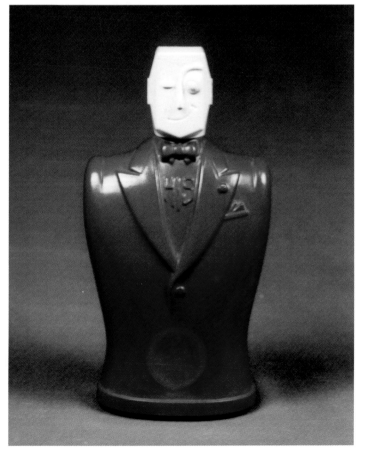

Lot #309. House for Men *HIS* clear glass bottle and white plastic stopper molded as a man in tuxedo with square, stylized face, 6.3" [15.9 cm], empty, [no label], the bottle entirely covered in maroon enamel, patent # molded on bottom. Est. $150.00-$250.00.

Lot #310. Roger and Gallet *Fleurs d'Amour* ['Flowers of Love'] clear glass bottle and stopper, 4.5" [11.4 cm], the bottle decorated with a beautiful label, faceted stopper, empty, label with an ascending angel carrying flowers, in its red box with an identical label. Est. $350.00-$450.00.

Lot #311. D'Vora green glass bottle and translucent green stopper, 2.4" [6.1 cm], of flask shape, empty, bottom molded *France*. Est. $100.00-$200.00.

Lot #312. Lucien Lelong *Tailspin* clear glass bottle and stopper, 2.8" [7.1 cm], a faceted octagonal bottle, with perfume and sealed, in its elegant beige box. Est. $150.00-$250.00.

Lot #313. Peggy Hoyt *Flowers* frosted glass bottle with a brilliant blue stopper, 3.5" [8.9 cm], names acid etched on the front of the bottle, unsigned. Est. $100.00-$200.00.

Lot #314. Matchabelli *Stradivari* clear glass bottle and stopper in the shape of a crown, 2.5" [6.4 cm], parts of crown enameled in gold, label on bottom, in its pink silk-lined box. Est. $200.00-$300.00.

Lot #315. Matchabelli *Duchess of York* clear glass bottle with gold enamel in the shape of a crown, 2.6" [6.5 cm], empty, in its light blue box. Est. $100.00-$200.00.

Lot #316. D'Orsay *Milord* clear glass bottle and stopper, 3.1" [7.9 cm], the famous octagonal shaped bottle in clear glass, label at center, in its original box. Est. $200.00-$300.00.

Lot #317. Rendes *Ting Shang* extremely rare clear glass perfume bottle and stopper, 2.7" [6.9 cm], in the form of a man's face, painted in yellow, red, white, and black, empty. This bottle is circa 1924-5 and is very rare. Est. $4,000.00-$5,000.00.

Lot #318. Lancôme *Tresor* ['Treasure'] clear crystal bottle and metal screw on stopper, 3.9" [9.9 cm], cut with many facets as a beautiful gemstone, in its orginal brilliant red box. Est. $1,000.00-$1,250.00.

Lot #319. Rochambeau *Fleurs Modernes* ['Modern Flowers'] frosted glass bottle in a metal holder, 3.5" [9 cm], designed in the French 1920's Art Deco style, the flowers painted in pale violet; circa 1920's. This model is quite rare. Est. $1,000.00-$1,200.00.

Lot #320. Vigny *Le Golliwogg* frosted glass bottle and black glass stopper, 2.6" to top of hair [6.6 cm], molded as a Golliwogg, apparently unopened, crisp label on front, in its box lined in brilliant pink silk. Est. $700.00-$900.00.

Lot #321. Ybry *Femme de Paris* ['Woman of Paris'], clear crystal bottle and stopper, 3.1" [7.8 cm] to top of stopper, gold label on front, near full and sealed, in its cream colored presentation box with gold tassel. Est. $800.00-$1,000.00.

Lot #322. Schiaparelli *Succes Fou* ['Smash Hit'] white glass leaf-form bottle and screw on stopper, 3.6" [9.1 cm], in the shape of a fig leaf, empty, the entire bottle enameled in green and gold, bottom molded *Schiaparelli*. Est. $700.00-$900.00.

Lot #323. Vigny *Le Golliwogg* clear glass bottle and black glass stopper molded as a Golliwogg, 3.5" [8.9 cm] to top of hair, full and sealed, with label in its original box of deep red satin, overall pristine condition. Est. $750.00-$1,000.00.

Lot #324. Hattie Carnegie clear glass bottle and stopper, 4.2" [10.7 cm], in the shape of a woman's head and shoulders, highlights in gold enamel, empty, name at the base of the bottle. Est. $300.00-$400.00.

Lot #325. Lancôme *Peut-Etre* ['Perhaps' but translated in Lancôme publicity as 'Who Knows...'] clear glass bottle and stopper, 4.7" [12 cm], both bottle and stopper in a star shape with eight points, full and sealed, gold metallic label at center, in a beautiful box decorated with a 17th century Florentine motif and a cupid and printed by Draeger; this was designed by Jean Sala and produced as a limited edition in 1943, the very darkest year of World War II. Est. $3,000.00-$4,000.00.

Lot #326. Schiaparelli *Sleeping* clear glass bottle and red flame stopper, 5.5" [14 cm], shaped as a candle, label at base, in its original box. Est. $400.00-$500.00.

Lot. #327. Hattie Carnegie *Carte Blanche* clear glass bottle and stopper, 3.4" [8.6 cm], in the shape of a woman's head and shoulders, name spelled out in raised letters at bottom and decorated in gold, label around neck and on bottom of bottle. This is a difficult size to find. Est. $500.00-$600.00.

Lot #328. Unidentified perfumer frosted glass bottle, inner stopper and head, in the shape of a sitting elephant, 3.5" [8.9 cm], tusks painted white, indistinctly marked on the bottom. Est. $400.00-$500.00.

Lot #329. Duvelle *Le Gui* ['Mistletoe'] green glass bottle and stopper, 3.2" [8.1 cm], of teardrop shape with a button stopper, empty, pretty metallic labels on front of bottle which is also decorated with pink bows, in its box covered with a graphic of Duvelle perfumes. Est. $250.00-$350.00.

Lot #330. Saint Cyr *Flêches d'Amour* ['Love Arrows'] clear glass bottle, inner stopper, and blue glass overcap, 4" [10.2 cm], the stopper molded with bands of gold and stars, empty, in its box which totally conceals the bottle and allows only the cap to be shown. Est. $250.00-$350.00.

Lot #331. Unidentified perfumer clear glass bottle and black glass stopper, 6.1" [15.5 cm], the dauber of the stopper is a nude hanging from a serpent's tail, bottom marked *France*. Est. $800.00-$1,000.00.

Lot #332. Bienaimé *Cuir de Russie* ['Russian Leather'] clear glass bottle and stopper, 2.6" [6.7 cm], the bottle designed as three oval tiers with scalloped edges, similar stopper, full and sealed, with its label, in its drop-front gold foil box decorated with Russian hunting scenes. Est. $250.00-$350.00.

Lot #333. Bienaimé *Caravane* clear glass bottle and stopper, 4" [10.2 cm], the bottle and stopper molded with facets, with perfume and sealed, in its lovely box of gold decorated with an oriental city of minarets. Est. $400.00-$500.00.

Lot #334. D'Orsay *Divine* clear glass bottle and stopper in an urn form, 7" [17.8 cm], the entirety molded with swirling lines, sealed, gold label around neck, bottom signed *D'Orsay* in acid, in its elegant box on which the name is spelled in a chain of flowers. Est. $500.00-$600.00.

Lot #335. Bryenne *Chu Chin Chow* blue glass bottle and overcap molded as a fat oriental man holding a fan and enameled in gold, his robe in dark blue with green dots, empty, inner stopper lacking, in its pagoda box [as is]; bottom marked *Bryenne Paris* in enamel and signed *C. K. Benda*. A lovely example of this model. Est. $3,000.00-$4,000.00.

Lot #336. Poiret *Moment Supreme* large size black bottle and stopper, 5.5" [14 cm], both bottle and stopper molded with flowers, with its label. Est. $100.00-$150.00.

Lot #337. D'Orsay *Rose d'Orsay* clear glass bottle and stopper, 3.1" [7.9 cm], of octagonal pillow form with ball stopper, full and sealed, gold label, in its box with a blue medallion of the Chevalier d'Orsay on the cover. Est. $200.00-$300.00.

Lot #338. Marquay *L'Elu* ['The Chosen'] clear glass bottle and stopper molded with a cut gemstone motif, 3.2" [8.1 cm], empty, gold label on front of bottle, in its elegant peach velvet evening bag with tasseled drawstrings and original box. Est. $350.00-$450.00.

Lot #339. Bourjois *Evening in Paris* large blue glass bottle and clear glass stopper, 4.2" [10.7 cm], the bottle of urn shape, the stopper molded as a fan, empty, silver label on the front, in its deluxe silver fabric box. Est. $300.00-$400.00.

Lot #340. Lionceau *Parfum pour Blondes* ['Perfume for Blondes'] green glass bottle and stopper, 3.2" [8.1 cm], the oval bottle molded front and back with leaves, label at center, bottom signed *Lionceau*. Est. $400.00-$500.00.

Lot #341. Molinard *Lutchou Quintessence de Fleurs* clear and gold glass bottle and stopper, 3" [7.6 cm], the gold parts molded with flowers, in its original box. Est. $150.00-$250.00.

Lot #342. House of Tre-Jur *Tre-Jur* frosted glass bottle and stopper in the form of a woman, 2.5" [6.3 cm]; stopper formed as the torso with a delicate long dauber intact; skirt is decorated with abstract symbols, name acid etched on bottom, empty. Est. $350.00-$450.00.

Lot #344. Jacques Griffe *Mistigri* clear glass bottle and stopper, 6.5" [16.5 cm], a beautifully designed bottle with a pedestal base and prism shape, full and sealed, name in gold enamel on front, bottom signed *Jacques Griffe* in white enamel, in its unusual box which opens like a flower. Est. $600.00-$800.00.

Lot #343. Richard Hudnut *Le Debut Vert* green glass octagonal bottle and stopper, 2.2" [5.6 cm], label on front, in its greenish box. Est. $600.00-$750.00.

Lot #345. Vigny *Echo Troublant* clear glass bottle and stopper, 2.4" [6 cm], bottle in a coat of arms shape, Vigny logo molded into stopper, full and sealed, thin gold label, in its box. Est. $200.00-$300.00.

Lot #346. Jeanne Lanvin *Arpege* black glass bottle and stopper, 3" [7.6 cm], of ball shape with a 'raspberry' stopper enameled in gold, signed *Lanvin Parfums* with the logo in gold on front, label on bottom, empty, in its original écru and black box. Est. $300.00-$400.00.

Lot #347. Karoff *Tap Cologne Carnation* barrel, 3.7" long [9.4 cm], label on side and bottom of barrel, with some perfume. Est. $50.00-$100.00.

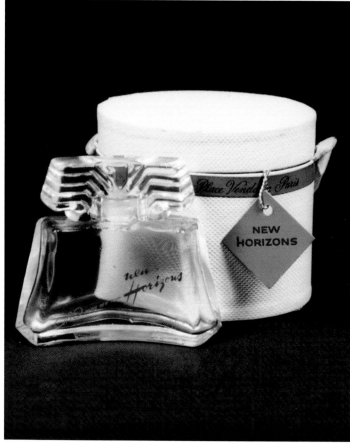

Lot #348. Ciro *New Horizons* clear glass bottle and stopper, 2.3" [5.8 cm], of curved shape, stopper in the form of a highly stylized eagle, names in enamel on front, in its hatbox with blue label. Est. $300.00-$400.00.

Lot #349. Richard Hudnut *Le Debut Noir* large size black glass perfume bottle and stopper, 2.5" [6.4 cm], gold label on bottom. Est. $400.00-$500.00.

Lot #350. Weil *Cobra* clear glass bottle and stopper of ovoid shape, 4.4" [11.2 cm], full and sealed, flower-form stopper, on its blue velvet plinth in its original box of black and gold. Est. $250.00-$350.00.

THE FRENCH MASTERS OF PERFUME BOTTLE DESIGN:
DÉPINOIX - JOLLIVET - LALIQUE - VIARD

Lot #351. Worth *Dans la Nuit* blue glass bottle and stopper, 5.2" [13.2 cm], circular base and stopper engraved *Dans la Nuit*, bottom faintly signed *R. Lalique*. Est. $200.00-$300.00.

Lot #352. Nina Ricci *Eau de Coeur Joie* clear glass bottle and stopper, 5" [12.7 cm], of flat round shape with a ball stopper, the letters *NR* on the neck of the bottle, with label, bottom signed *Lalique*. Est. $150.00-$250.00.

Lot #353. R. Lalique *Le Parisien* frosted glass atomizer, 7.3" [18.5 cm], the base covered with nudes who are playing with garlands of wreaths, metal signed *S.G.D.G.,* bottom signed *R. Lalique.* Est. $400.00-$600.00.

Lot #354. Worth *Sans Adieu* brilliant emerald green glass bottle and stopper of columnar shape, 4.2" [10.7 cm], the stopper molded as a series of seven rings [the last one is the lip of the bottle], signed *R. Lalique* in the mold. Utt #W-8. Est. $500.00-$650.00.

Lot #355. Large perfume atomizer, 5.1" [13 cm], the glass bottle entirely decorated with classical maidens in various poses, bottom molded *Made in France* and *R. Lalique.* Est. $800.00-$1,000.00.

Lot #356. Guerlain *Bouquet de Faunes* frosted glass bottle, 4.3" [10 cm], molded as an urn with four sides decorated with faces of a woman or satyr on each corner, bottle molded *Guerlain France,* unsigned [as one would expect for this bottle]. Est. $750.00-$1,000.00.

Lot #357. Jay Thorpe & Co. *Jaytho* clear and frosted glass bottle and stopper, 4.0" [10.2 cm], the entire bottle molded as a bouquet of tulips and the stopper as a bud, rich amber patina, *Jaytho* molded vertically on front, bottom molded *R. Lalique.* Utt #JT-1. Est. $1,000.00-$1,250.00.

Lot #358. Jay Thorpe & Co. *Jaytho* clear and frosted glass bottle and stopper, 6" [15.2 cm], the bottle molded as a bouquet of tulips and the stopper as a bud, rich amber patina, *Jaytho* molded vertically on the front. Est. $1,000.00-$1,250.00.

Lot #359. Worth *Imprudence* clear glass bottle and stopper in a design of concentric rings, 3.5" [8.9 cm], stopper with the original of two designs for this bottle, label on bottom, signed *R. L.* in the mold; a large size for this bottle. Est. $800.00-$1,000.00.

Lot #360. Houbigant *Le Temps des Lilas* ['Lilac Time'] clear glass bottle and stopper, 3.3" [8.4 cm], the oval shape decorated with a design of molded vertical lines and spirals in rows, names in enamel near base, molded signature *R. Lalique*. Utt #H-2 [1922]. Est. $1,250.00-$1,750.00.

Lot #361. Worth *Vers Toi* clear and frosted glass bottle and stopper, 2.9" [7.4 cm], the bottle of flower-pot shape embellished with rows of frosted chevrons at bottom, at the neck, and on the stopper, empty, label on shoulder, molded *R. Lalique* on bottom. Est. $400.00-$700.00.

Lot #362. Coty *Chypre* large bottle with a shell motif on the sides, 8" [20.3 cm], the stopper designed as two serpents, dark blue patina overall, unsigned. Est. $1,000.00-$1,250.00.

Lot #363. Worth *Je Reviens* huge size dark blue bottle and turquoise stopper, 11.3" [28.7 cm] the bottle entirely molded as a column with vertical ribs with steps at the top evoking a skyscraper, bottom molded *Lalique*. Utt #W-6. Est. $800.00-$1,000.00.

Lot #364. Maison Lalique *Telline* frosted glass bottle and stopper, 3.8" [9.7 cm], the bottle in the form of a large shell, the stopper molded as a smaller one, very tiny flake to the stopper, signed in the mold *R. Lalique*. Utt #ML-508. Est. $1,250.00-$1,500.00.

Lot #365. Maison Lalique *Hélène* clear and frosted glass eau de toilette bottle of very huge size, 9" [22.9 cm], with inner spritzer stopper and overcap; each tableau molded with classical women with scarves patinated dark brown, signed *Lalique* in block letters. Utt #ML-2. Est. $1,500.00-$2,000.00.

Lot #366. René Lalique brule-parfum *Sirènes* a beautiful perfume lamp 6.7" [17 cm], a swirl of mermaids cascading around, stopper with floral motif, the entirety frosted, possibly unsigned. Est. $3,500.00-$4,000.00.

Lot #367. D'Orsay set of four bottles and powder box: *Le Dandy, Ambre, Toujours Fidele, Mystere,* set of four bottles, each 2.4" [6.1 cm], with a kind of rope design which all fit together like pieces of an elaborate puzzle with powder jar at center, [two perfumes with very tiny holes] in their elaborate glass box with the D'Orsay coat of arms at center. *According to the Utt book, there is only one complete set, obviously beside this one.* Est. $15,000.00-$18,000.00.

Lot #368. Roger & Gallet *Pavots d'Argent*['Silver Poppies'] clear glass bottle and stopper, 3.3" [8.4 cm], bottle molded in the form of two overlapping open poppies, stopper also molded as a flower, with perfume and still sealed, label on back, in its pink and silver box, signed in the mold faintly *R. Lalique.* Est. $2,500.00-$3,000.00.

Lot #369. Nina Ricci *Farouche* clear glass bottle and stopper, 2.7" [6.9 cm], of urn shape with octagonal stopper, name in gold enamel on front, bottom signed *Lalique,* in its smart red box. Est. $100.00-$175.00.

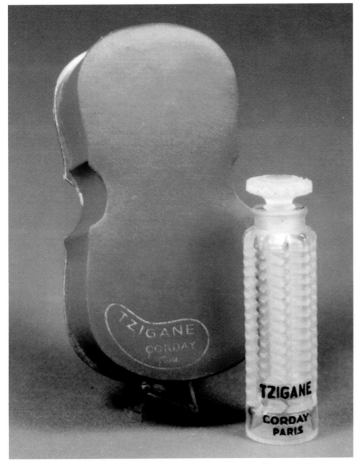

Lot #370. Corday *Tzigane* clear and frosted glass bottle and stopper, 3.8" [9.6 cm], indented zigzag design on a columnar form, names in black enamel, empty, bottom signed *R. Lalique,* in its violin-shaped box covered in deep red satin. Utt #Cor-1. Est. $1,500.00-$2,000.00.

Lot #371. Forvil *Narcisse* clear glass bottle and stopper, 2.6" [6.6 cm], the bottle molded with cascading bands of leaves, empty, gold label, signed *R. Lalique* in the mold, in its smart red and black box decorated in the Art Deco manner. Est. $3,000.00-$4,000.00.

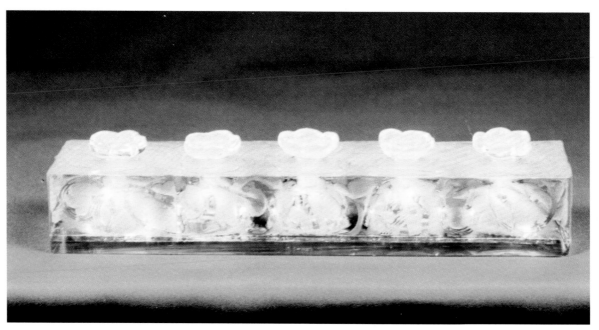

Lot #372. D'Orsay *Les Fleurs* clear and frosted glass tester bar for five fragrances, 8.8" x 2" x 1.8" [22.3 x 5.1 x 4.5 cm], entirely molded with a design of thorny branches, with the word *D'Orsay* spelled out as a part of the design on one side, the stoppers shaped as flowers and each stopper with a dauber and with the name of each fragrance molded in the center of the flower, numbered *1 Chypre; 2 Fleur de France; 3 Les Fleurs; 4 Le Chevalier; 5 Le Lys,* all with daubers, signed *Lalique* in the mold at the top. Utt Fig. 112. Est. $2,000.00-$2,500.00.

Lot #373. R. Lalique *Roger* brown glass box, 5.2" diameter [13.2 cm], molded all over with birds and grapevines and eleven polished circles, molded *Lalique* on the side and *R. Lalique* on the bottom; seen in the 1932 catalogue. Est. $800.00-$1,000.00.

Lot #374. Worth *Requête* ['Request'] clear glass bottle and stopper, 3.6" [9 cm], of flat round shape with a scallop motif enameled in blue, full and sealed with original double tag labels, initial *"W"* impressed in stopper, bottom signed *Lalique* in the mold; in its cream-colored box. Utt #W-105. Est. $1,000.00-$1,250.00.

Lot #375. Sabino opalescent glass box, 6.4" [16.3 cm], beautifully molded with three mermaids with interlocking hands, signed *Sabino Paris* in the mold. Est. $500.00-$750.00.

Lot #376. Rosine *Violette* clear glass bottle and stopper in the shape of a key, 3.9" [10 cm], a gold design around the bottle, red and white label at base. Est. $500.00-$600.00.

Lot #377. Small French atomizer bottle, 4.5" [11.4 cm], fashioned of flowers with interlocking rays as their petals, new ball and tassel, patinated in light blue with black highlights, unmarked. Est. $300.00-$450.00.

Lot #378. Val St. Lambert covered box, 4.7" [12 cm], the cover molded with the image of a mother and child, signed *Val St. Lambert Belgique* on cover and on bottom of box. Est. $200.00-$300.00.

Lot #379. Isabey *Ambre de Carthage* clear glass bottle and stopper, 2.3" [6.6 cm], covered with orange enamel which cascades downward, by Julien Viard. Est. $800.00-$1,000.00.

Lot #380. Les Parfums de Malyne *Le Bar Claire de Lune* clear and partially frosted glass bottle and stopper, both bottle and stopper molded with swirls of flowers and leaves and patinated blue, empty, pretty label on front, in its box lined in satin and signed *Malyne* on the front. Not found in current reference works. Est. $1,750.00-$2,250.00.

Lot #381. DuBarry *Arcadia* clear and frosted glass bottle and stopper, 5" [12.7 cm], the four-sided bottle designed with panels of masks near the top, the stopper molded with leaves, charcoal patina, empty, by J. Viard, unsigned, in its satin-lined green box. Est. $2,000.00-$2,500.00.

Lot #382. Unidentified clear and black glass bottle and stopper, 2.6" [6.6 cm], molded as a snuff bottle with a black coral motif, full and sealed, bottom signed *J. Viard*, in its original holder and box with oriental motifs. Est. $2,500.00-$3,500.00.

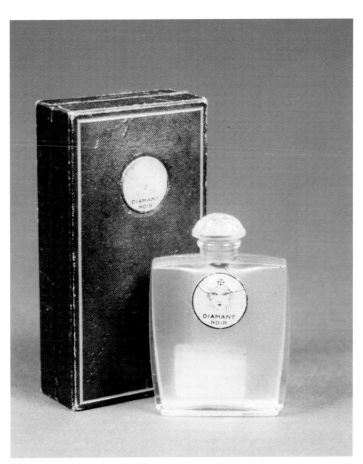

Lot #383. Isabey *Bleu de Chine* ['China Blue'] clear and frosted glass bottle and stopper, 2.9" [7.4 cm], the bottle molded with eight panels of flowers and leaves, narrow clear glass vertical windows, stopper with conforming design, the designs embellished with blue and orange enamel, full and sealed, apparently unsigned, in its superb box whose side opens to reveal the bottle. Est. $10,000.00-$12,000.00.

Lot #384. Lydès *Diamant Noir* ['Black Diamond'] clear glass bottle and stopper, 2.7" [6.9 cm], the stopper molded with flowers and patinated amber, empty, pretty gold and green label on front of bottle and on box, in its brown and gold box signed *Lydès* on the inside, unsigned. This fragrance is not listed in current reference works. Est. $750.00-$1,000.00.

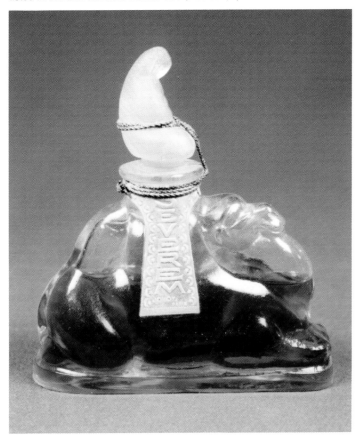

Lot #385. Lydes *Berylis*, 2.8" [7.1 cm], the bottle of elongated hexagonal form, the stopper a maiden, with a necklace of fur, bottom signed France; by Julien Viard. Est. $1,500.00-$2,000.00.

Lot #386. Jovoy *Severem* clear glass camel with a figural robed rider in frosted glass, 3.5" [8.9 cm], full and sealed, bottom signed *© Lordonnais 1922 France*. Est. $1,500.00-$2,000.00.

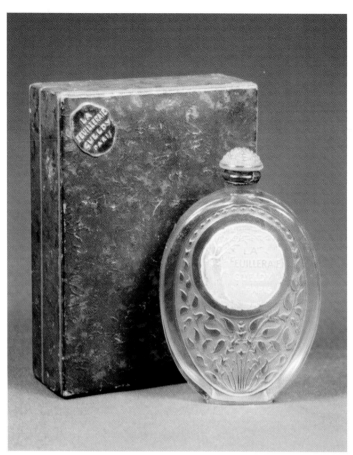

Lot #387. Gueldy *La Feuilleraie* clear glass bottle and stopper, 3.7" [9.4 cm], the oval bottle molded with leaves and a very big gold label showing a tree, very tiny bruise at the base, in its superb condition box, also with a label. Est. $3,500.00-$4,500.00.

Lot #388. Lubin *Eva* clear and frosted glass bottle and stopper, 3.7" [9.4 cm], the bottle of flattened round shape with four garlands of flowers molded down the sides and which form four feet on the bottom, the stopper molded as Eve crouched atop a coiled snake, amber patina, full and sealed, unsigned, by J. Viard. Est. $2,000.00-$2,500.00.

Lot #389. Agnel *Fête de Nuit* black glass bottle and stopper, 3.1" [7.8 cm], shaped almost like a bell with six sides, full and sealed, by Julien Viard. Est. $1,500.00-$2,500.00.

Lot #390. Richard Hudnut *Fadette* clear glass bottle and stopper, 4" [10.2 cm], the stopper a classical maiden with flowers, label on bottom, part of dauber broken, signed *Made in France*. Est. $1,000.00-$1,250.00.

Lot #391. Benoit *Ange de Gloire* ['Angel of Glory'] clear glass bottle and stopper, 5" [12.7 cm], the sides beautifully molded with flowers, the stopper a kneeling maiden with hexagonal cap, the sides molded with flowers and patinated green, label on front, unsigned. Not seen in the printed literature. Est. $8,000.00-$12,000.00.

Lot #392. Rosine *Coeur en Folie* ['Heart in Madness'] red glass bottle and frosted glass stopper shaped as wings, 1.5" tall [3.8 cm], full and sealed, label on top, in its red heart-shaped box. This is a superb perfume presentation, and very few may exist with the box. Est. $15,000.00-$20,000.00.

Lot #393. T. Jones *Gai Paris* beautiful bottle molded with trees on the sides, 4" [10.2 cm], the bottle molded with two different Parisian scenes and patinated dark green, names in gold on front, *T. Jones* label on bottom, stopper frozen and hairline at neck. Est. $1,000.00-$1,500.00.

Lot #394. Myrurgia *Maja* rare clear glass bottle and frosted glass stopper, 5.4" [13.7 cm], the stopper designed as an architectural column, red and gold label, some perfume, Spanish tax stamps on the reverse side, in its beautiful but very worn box; written on the sides of the box in stylized letters are the words *En un solo perfume todas las flores de España* ['In one perfume all the flowers of Spain'], unsigned. Est. $1,500.00-$2,000.00.

CZECHOSLOVAKIAN PERFUME BOTTLES

Lot #395. Metal clad purse bottle, 2.1" [5.3 cm], inset with a glass cameo of a goddess, encased in metal with blue stones, signed on the neck with a tag *Czechoslovakia*. Est. $125.00-$200.00.

Lot #396. Lot of three clear crystal bottles and pink stoppers in their pink crystal holder, bottle height 2" [5.1 cm], daubers lacking, bottom of each bottle signed *Czechoslovakia.* Est. $125.00-$200.00.

Lot #397. Clear crystal bottle of round shape, 3.7" [9.4 cm], the bottle and stopper molded with steps and decorated with an abstract motif in red and black, signed *Czechoslovakia.* Est. $150.00-$200.00.

Lot #398. Tiny purse bottle decorated with colored stones, 2" [5.1 cm], larger lavendar stone in the screw on stopper, unsigned. Est. $200.00-$300.00.

Lot #399. Black crystal miniature bottle with metal cap and glass stopper with long dauber, 2.1" [5.3 cm], covered in a frieze of metal and red and black jewels, bottom signed *Made in Czechoslovakia.* Est. $200.00-$300.00.

Lot #400. Metal clad glass perfume bottle and stopper, 3" [7.6 cm], the exterior highly decorated with rhinestones, signed *Czechoslovakia* on the neck. Est. $150.00-$250.00.

Lot #401. Miniature bottle of glass with metal and bakelite top, 2.6" [6.6 cm], two beaded glass figures hanging from the top, bottom marked *IRice*. Est. $100.00-$175.00.

Lot #402. Jeweled purse bottle and stopper, 2.6" [6.5 cm], beautifully decorated with blue and clear stones, signed on a tag at the neck *Czechoslovakia*. Est. $200.00-$300.00.

Lot #403. Clear crystal bottle and light yellow crystal stopper, 4" [10.1 cm], with its tiny dauber, bottom signed *Czechoslovakia* in an oval. Est. $100.00-$200.00.

Lot #404. Clear crystal bottle with metal overcap and inner glass stopper with long dauber, 2" [5.1 cm], covered in a frieze of metal and green and pink jewels, unsigned. Est. $200.00-$300.00.

Lot #405. Jeweled Czech pink crystal bottle and clear stopper, 4.5" [11.4 cm], the bottle decorated with a pink carved stone and pearls, bottom signed *Made in Czechoslovakia.* Est. $200.00-$300.00.

Lot #406. Clear crystal bottle with metal overcap and inner glass stopper with long dauber, 2" [5.1 cm], covered in a frieze of metal and green and blue jewels, signed *Made in Czechoslovakia.* Est. $200.00-$300.00.

Lot #407. Lot of 4: Jeweled Czechoslovakian bottle with violet stones and pearls, 2.5" [6.3 cm], signed by metal tag; Czechoslovakian hexagonal bottle with blue stones, 1.8" [4.6 cm], signed with metal tag; triangular bottle with blue stone; metal bottle with lily of the valley. Four items. Est. $200.00-$300.00.

Lot #408. Green crystal atomizer bottle, 4.5" [11.4 cm], the front molded with an Art Deco maiden amid flowers, apparently unsigned. Est. $300.00-$400.00.

Lot #409. Clear and frosted crystal box and cover, 4.4" x 3.7" [11.2 x 9.4 cm], the cover with two male figures struggling against cloth, bottom signed *Czechoslovakia* in an oval. Est. $350.00-$500.00.

Lot #410. Tall green and clear crystal bottle and stopper, 7.5" [19 cm], the bottle resting on a diamond shaped pedestal with broad geometric facets, dauber lacking, signed *Czechoslovakia* in a circle. Est. $150.00-$250.00.

Lot #411. Clear crystal bottle and stopper, 6.4" [16.3 cm], the stopper with many facets, the bottle also highly cut and with four feet, signed *Czechoslovakia* on one foot. Est. $150.00-$250.00.

Lot #412. Green crystal bottle and clear stopper, 6.1" [15.5 cm], the base cut with a cross-hatch design, the stopper cut with roses and a trellis, dauber lacking, signed *Czechoslovakia* in a circle. Est. $200.00-$300.00.

Lot #413. Massive clear crystal bottle and stopper, 6.3" [16 cm], of simple geometric form with stopper conforming to bottle, dauber lacking, signed *Czechoslovakia* in an oval. Est. $150.00-$250.00.

Lot #414. Clear crystal bottle and stopper, 4.8" [12.2 cm], the stopper intaglio cut with a woman and her dog, with its dauber, signed *Czechoslovakia* in an oval. Est. $250.00-$350.00.

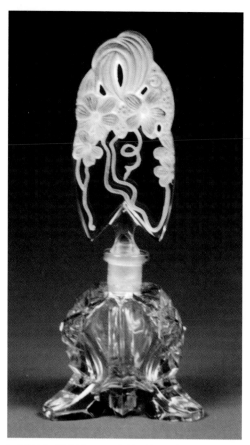

Lot #415. Tall blue crystal bottle and stopper, 8.6" [21.8 cm], triangular cut base, stopper molded with flowers and vines and with cut-out portions, dauber lacking, bottom signed *Czechoslovakia* in a line. Est. $600.00-$750.00.

Lot #416. Yellow crystal bottle and clear crystal stopper, 5.3" [13.5 cm], the bottle made to look like an inkwell with a tall feather stopper, signed *Czechoslovakia* in an oval. Est. $250.00-$350.00.

Lot #417. Clear crystal bottle and stopper, 5.5" [14 cm], the bottle with four feet, the stopper intaglio cut with the face of a goddess in profile, dauber lacking, signed *Czechoslovakia*. Est. $200.00-$300.00.

Lot #418. Clear bottle and pink crystal stopper, 6.5" [16.5 cm], the stopper molded with four flowers, with its dauber, bottom signed *Made in Czechoslovakia* in a circle. Est. $300.00-$400.00.

Lot #419. Large clear crystal bottle with pink top, 5.7" [14.5 cm], identical geometric pattern cut into both bottle and stopper, dauber lacking, bottom signed *Czechoslovakia* in a circle. Est. $150.00-$250.00.

Lot #420. Clear crystal bottle and black stopper, 4.9" [12.4 cm], a star motif cut into both sides of the bottle and the front of the stopper, dauber lacking, probably unsigned. Est. $100.00-$175.00.

Lot #421. Black crystal bottle and clear crystal stopper, 5.4" [13.7 cm], the bottle designed in the shape of a star, the stopper also cut with rays, with its dauber, signed *Czechoslovakia*. Est. $350.00-$450.00.

Lot #422. Clear crystal bottle and stopper, 6.2" [15.7 cm], of decanter shape with leaves and berries enameled in black on four panels and on stopper, unsigned. Est. $200.00-$300.00.

Lot #423. Black crystal bottle with clear stopper, 6.4" [16.3 cm], the bottle molded with frosted Art Deco motifs, simple stopper, dauber lacking, signed *Czechoslovakia*. Est. $250.00-$350.00.

Lot #424. Clear crystal bottle and stopper, 6.3" [16 cm], the bottle and stopper highly cut with a geometric motif, dauber lacking, signed *Czechoslovakia* in a circle. Est. $200.00-$300.00.

Lot #425. Clear crystal bottle and stopper, 5.7" [14.5 cm], an intricately cut bottle with a small bridge at the bottom, the stopper cut with facets and intaglio cut with birds carrying a bower of flowers, with its dauber, unsigned. Est. $300.00-$400.00.

Lot #426. Clear crystal perfume bottle and stopper, 7.2" [18.3 cm], the stopper formed as a very large open loop, cut on both sides, bottom signed *Czechoslovakia*. Est. $300.00-$400.00.

Lot #427. Cameo style clear and frosted crystal bottle and stopper, 7.3" [18.5 cm], the bottle with four prominent feet, the stopper molded with the face of a woman in a low cut dress and a pearl necklace, dauber lacking, signed *Czechoslovakia* in a circle. Est. $500.00-$650.00.

Lot #428. Clear crystal bottle and stopper, 4.8" [12.2 cm], the bottle on four feet, the stopper also of rectangular shape intaglio cut with an oval cameo of a 19th century lady in a bonnet with a bow, dauber lacking, signed *Czechoslovakia* in an oval. Est. $500.00-$600.00.

Lot #429. Clear crystal bottle and blue crystal stopper, 5.3" [13.4 cm], the bottle of unusual shape and highly cut, the stopper in the shape of a starburst and with its dauber, unsigned. Est. $250.00-$350.00.

Lot #430. Extremely large clear crystal bottle and stopper of tiara form, 7.2" [18.3 cm], the bottle and stopper cut with conforming abstract motifs, dauber lacking, signed *Czechoslovakia* in a circle. Est. $600.00-$900.00.

Lot #431. Premier clear crystal bottle and stopper, 7.6" [19.3 cm], the base highly cut, the stopper with a figure of a woman admiring a bunch of flowers, parts of stopper cut out and parts frosted, signed with Premier label and Czechoslovakian label. Est. $1,000.00-$1,250.00.

Lot #432. Clear crystal bottle and stopper, 7.1" [18 cm], the bottle cut in a butterfly motif, the stopper intaglio cut with a lady and peacock, dauber lacking, bottom apparently unsigned. Est. $600.00-$800.00.

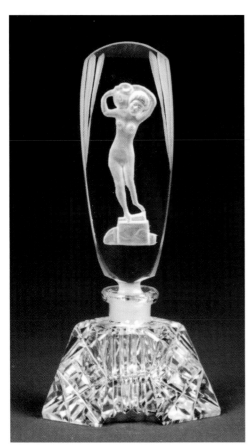

Lot #433. Clear crystal perfume bottle and stopper, 6.3" [16 cm], the bottle resting on two feet, the stopper with its dauber and showing a maiden carrying a large jug, signed *Czechoslovakia* in an oval. Est. $500.00-$600.00.

Lot #434. Clear crystal bottle and stopper, 6.6" [16.8 cm], the bottle highly carved and resting on three feet, the stopper in the form of a figure eight with a wreath of flowers, bottom signed *Made in Czechoslovakia*. Est. $200.00-$300.00.

Lot #435. Large clear crystal bottle and stopper, 7.2" [18.3 cm], the stopper intaglio cut with a woman descending stairs and holding a bouquet [dauber lacking], signed with a silver label *Bohemia Crystal Made in Czechoslovakia*. Est. $400.00-$600.00.

Lot #436. Clear crystal bottle and stopper, 6.2" [15.7 cm], the stopper intaglio cut with three roses, the bottle highly cut, with its dauber, signed *Czechoslovakia* in a circle. Est. $250.00-$350.00.

Lot #437. Clear crystal bottle and stopper, 5.1" [13 cm], the stopper intaglio cut with two heads stylized in the Art Deco manner, with its dauber, bottom signed *Czechoslovakia* in a line. Est. $250.00-$350.00.

Lot #438. Large clear crystal bottle and stopper, 7.3" [18.5 cm], the bottle roughly of hexagonal form and cut on the bottom, the stopper a nude with cut out portions, dauber lacking, bottom signed *Czechoslovakia* in an oval. Est. $1,500.00-$2,000.00.

Lot #439. Massive clear crystal bottle and yellow crystal stopper, 6.5" [16.5 cm], the stopper intaglio cut with flowers and in the form of a partial tiara, bottom of bottle apparenly unsigned. Est. $300.00-$400.00.

Lot #440. Peach colored crystal bottle and stopper, 5.9" [15 cm], the bottle cut with a geometric motif, dauber lacking, tongue of stopper with bruise, unsigned. Est. $100.00-$200.00.

Lot #441. Peach crystal bottle and stopper, 5.4" [13.7 cm], the stopper with pink dauber features two children playing music to a dancing woman, signed with the Hoffman butterfly. Est. $500.00-$600.00.

Lot #442. Pink crystal bottle and clear crystal stopper, 6.3" [16 cm], both base and stopper are highly cut in a church window pattern, with its dauber, bottom signed *Czechoslovakia* in an oval. Est. $250.00-$350.00.

Lot #443. Unusual Hoffman bottle of black crystal and a clear stopper, 5.4" [13.7 cm], both the bottle and the stopper an open rose, leaning backward, bottom molded with the Hoffman butterfly. Est. $1,000.00-$1,250.00.

Lot #444. Gigantic clear crystal bottle and stopper, 9.8" [24.9 cm], the stopper with the figure of a woman amid flowers, many cut-out portions, highly cut bottom, with its dauber, apparently unsigned. Est. $1,000.00-$1,500.00.

Lot #445. Gigantic clear and frosted crystal bottle and stopper, 9" [22.9 cm], the sides of the bottle molded with grapes and leaves, with red patina, unsigned. Est. $400.00-$600.00.

Lot #446. Hoffman light smokey crystal bottle and stopper, 6.3" [16 cm], the stopper, with its dauber, featuring a classical maiden climbing uphill, signed with the Hoffman butterfly. Est. $1,000.00-$1,250.00.

Lot #447. Clear crystal bottle and red crystal stopper, 4.4" [11.2 cm], the bottle cut with diamond facets, the stopper molded in the form of a cube standing on one point, dauber lacking, unsigned. Est. $400.00-$500.00.

Lot #448. Blue crystal bottle and stopper, 4.9" [12.4 cm], the base highly cut in a geometric fashion, bottom apparently unsigned. Est. $300.00-$400.00.

Lot #449. Huge size clear crystal bottle and stopper, 8.6" [21.8 cm], the huge stopper features a frosted butterfly atop a stylized flower, dauber lacking, signed *Czechoslovakia* in an oval. Est. $500.00-$600.00.

Lot #450. Clear crystal bottle and stopper, 5.7" [14.5 cm], the stopper intaglio cut with flowers, signed *Czechoslovakia* in a circle. Est. $150.00-$250.00.

Lot #451. Rose colored crystal perfume bottle and stopper, 6.5" [16.5 cm], of beautiful tiara form with a frosted panel of roses at center, with its dauber, unsigned. Est. $400.00-$600.00.

Lot #452. Yellow crystal bottle and stopper, 6.2" [15.7 cm], the intricate stopper with a cut out portion, with its dauber, signed *Czechoslovakia* and with original paper label. Est. $300.00-$400.00.

Lot #453. Smoke colored crystal bottle and stopper, both the bottle and stopper molded with an arch-shaped design, both intaglio cut with similar abstract motifs, with its dauber, unsigned. Est. $300.00-$400.00.

Lot #454. Hoffman clear crystal bottle and translucent blue stopper, 6.1" [15.5 cm], the rectangular bottle beautifully translucent, the stopper a nude, signed with the Hoffman butterfly. Est. $5,000.00-$6,000.00.

Lot #455. Interesting motif two color crystal bottle and stopper, red on dark red, 3" [7.6 cm], a design of leaves and berries and an overlay of red, signed *Czechoslovakia*. Est. $800.00-$1,000.00.

Lot #456. Clear crystal bottle and stopper, 6.6" [16.7 cm], the bottle in a fan motif and covered in green jewels, the stopper intaglio molded with a nude and flowers, dauber lacking, signed by Morlee label. Est. $2,500.00-$3,500.00.

Lot #457. Blue crystal bottle and stopper, 8.5" [21.6 cm], the bottle highly cut, the stopper beautifully shaped as a nude emerging from a flower, bottom signed with Morlee label and *Czechoslovakia* in an oval. Est. $3,500.00-$4,500.00.

Lot #458. Ingrid smokey topaz crystal bottle and stopper, 5.4" [13.7 cm], the bottle molded on both sides with a nude against a backdrop of leaves, conforming stopper with its long dauber, bottom signed *Ingrid Czechoslovakia*. Est. $1,000.00-$1,250.00.

Lot #459. Black crystal bottle with a clear and frosted stopper, 7.5" [19 cm], the bottle shaped like a fountain with cascades of water, the stopper an Art Deco nude on one side with cascades of water on the other side, dauber lacking, unsigned. Est. $3,000.00-$4,000.00.

Lot #460. Violet jeweled crystal bottle and stopper, 5.5" [14 cm], the bottle cut as a fan and bearing green jewels, the back of the bottle cut with the same flower that is on the stopper, signed *Czechoslovakia*. Est. $400.00-$500.00.

Lot #461. Violet crystal bottle with clear glass stopper, 2.8" [7.1 cm], the bottle shaped as a butterfly, the front of the bottle covered with a frieze of metal with pearls and violet stones, signed *Czechoslovakia* on the neck and [faintly] on bottom. Est. $350.00-$500.00.

Lot #462. Huge size smoke crystal bottle and clear crystal top, 9.9" [25.1 cm], of circular form with roses intaglio cut into the front, the stopper also cut with roses, no dauber, signed *Czechoslovakia* in a line. Est. $400.00-$600.00.

Lot #463. Violet crystal bottle and stopper, 6" [15.2 cm], the bottle of unusual form, cut with various motifs and partially frosted, the stopper two baby angels standing on a flower, dauber lacking, unsigned. Est. $350.00-$450.00.

Lot #464. Pink crystal bottle and stopper, 7.5" [19 cm], the base with nine protruding feet, the stopper molded as a nude holding up the world symbolized by an opaque crystal globe, with its dauber, bottom signed *Czechoslovakia*. Est. $6,000.00-$7,500.00.

Lot #465. Hoffman opaque orange red crystal bottle and black crystal stopper, 5.1" [13 cm], the bottle molded with two Art Deco nudes on both sides of the bottle, the black stopper with its original dauber, signed with the Hoffman butterfly. Est. $6,000.00-$7,500.00.

Lot #466. Large green jeweled crystal bottle and stopper, 6.3" [16 cm], the stopper with three fanciful flowers and cut through, the bottle encased with jewels in metal, signed *Czechoslovakia* in a circle. Est. $1,000.00-$1,250.00.

Lot #467. Opaque malachite perfume bottle and stopper, 6" [15.2 cm], the bottle molded with a nude on both sides of the bottle, the stopper molded with a bird, dauber lacking, bottom signed indistinctly *Czechoslovakia*. Est. $1,000.00-$1,500.00.

Lot #468. Yellow crystal bottle and frosted glass stopper, 7" [17.8 cm], the stopper a graceful statue of a maiden, the bottle a deep rich yellow, dauber lacking, bottom signed *Czechoslovakia* in a circle. Est. $2,000.00-$2,500.00.

Lot #469. Sumptuous black crystal powder box, rouge pot, and lipstick carrier, 10.2" x 6.4" [26 x 16.3 cm], the lid of powder box and rouge pot in amber crystal, the black glass molded with eight nudes all in voluptuous poses, base encrusted with twenty green crystal stones, side inscribed *Austria*. Est. $6,000.00-$8,000.00.

Lot #470. Ingrid opaque dark reddish brown and red crystal bottle and stopper, 6" [15.2 cm], the bottle with four sides and embellished with a nude in red fanning herself, the stopper with flowers, lip of the bottle enameled gold, with its dauber, bottom signed *Ingrid* and with gold label. Probably the finest Czechoslovakian bottle we have ever offered. Est. $12,000.00-$15,000.00.